The We
Past and

Lycanthropy's Lost
History and Modern
Devolution

TM

By Maegan A. Stebbins

In memory of my Grandma Barbara.
I love you, always, and I miss you.

Copyright © 2017-2021 Maegan A. Stebbins

ISBN-13: 978-1-949227-02-4

Maegan A. Stebbins was born in Virginia in 1993 and has Master's and bachelor's degrees in English from Virginia Polytechnic Institute and State University, with minors in History and Medieval Studies. She is the co-creator of the Wulfgard medieval fantasy universe, the Nova Refuge sci-fi universe, the creator of other universes, and author of several books, including *The Prophecy of the Six* series. Her fiction focuses primarily, but not exclusively, on transformation and what it means to be human, and she continues to research folklore, mythology, and popular culture, with a focus on monsters, especially werewolves.

Cover design and logo by Justin R. R. Stebbins

Visit online at:
www.maverickwerewolf.com

Author's Note

Before you continue, it is important to note that the following work was written, edited, and completed in 2017. This work has not been edited to feature additional scholarship or mention of any popular culture works beyond 2017, when it was originally published. Also note this is not by any means intended to cover every single piece of werewolf media. This was written and published under time and length constraints, as a Master's degree thesis.

I previously announced my plans to rename this book to *Death of the Werewolf*, but I discovered shortly thereafter that, where a shorter and less refined edition of this study was published online at my alma mater's website under the title *The Werewolf: Past and Future*, it had received several thousand downloads so far and has already been cited elsewhere. Thus, the original title has remained.

Regarding its original publication date, virtually nothing has changed about to the topics at hand. Regardless, please bear in mind while reading that some language and references to popular culture may seem somewhat dated now.

Preface

For as long as I can remember, I have been fascinated by werewolves. I cannot recall exactly how or when I first learned of werewolves or what made me like them so, but it was as young as four or six years old, since I know I was fully obsessed with the concept of werewolves by the time I was seven. My preoccupation with werewolves was strengthened – but not started – by my many years spent roleplaying online in the video game *Neverwinter Nights*, on a server called The Nameless Land, where I was allowed to play as creatures such as werewolves, demons, and dragons; to this day, I thank that game, the administration of the server (especially you, Alex), and the playerbase of the server for greatly fostering the interest I now have in writing and folklore, and for helping me to explore many of the characters I still write about today.

Ironically, most all werewolf media frustrates me, be it insistently comical with dog-people "werewolves" or meaningless celebrations of gore, which makes it even more difficult to pinpoint precisely when and where they captivated me. Perhaps it all began with strange dreams I began to have about a white werewolf, as these are the earliest memories I have of lycanthropes as a concept. The fact that I do not enjoy the overwhelming majority of werewolf portrayals of any recent entertainment history provides another reason why the topic of this study is so very important to me.

Whatever the case may be with the where and when and how I became obsessed with werewolves, the fact remains that I find werewolves fascinating, and I always will. To me, werewolves represent not only, on the surface, the "coolest" possible monster or creature imaginable, but also they hold potential for a staggering variety of deep explorations of almost countless themes. Even during my childhood, I knew I wanted to write something to explore both the potential of werewolves in fiction, and to present to the world the rich history of werewolf legends. In my opinion, as you will see in this book, werewolves have incredible untapped potential in stories, especially since entertainment today has utterly forgotten their legendary roots in favor of various modern contrivances by horror movie writers (not that every single invention of theirs is dislikable at all, such as the sensitivity to silver, which can – at times – create for an interesting aspect in a story) and also turning werewolves into walking dog jokes that are never to be taken seriously.

Ultimately, Charlotte F. Otten, the author of *A Lycanthropy Reader*, may have stated it best in the end of her introduction,

> Although no one today believes in actual physical metamorphosis of a human being into a wolf, there is no doubt that a werewolf, a lycanthrope, whether in a clinic, forest, courtroom, in legend or myth, in non-fictional or allegorical accounts, evokes terror or pity in the viewer or reader. To admit the werewolf into human consciousness is to admit the need to examine the moral underpinnings of society.[1]

I could, of course, continue elaborating upon my lifelong belief that werewolves are, in two words, the best. For the time being, however, I hope this study will suffice in providing much useful information and inspiring some of the

---

[1] Otten 15

thought that modern audiences and creators alike so desperately need to consider.

In closing, I will remind you for a final time that this thesis in its entirety was written in 2017 and not entirely updated for years beyond it to 2021. It does not address more recent releases in terms of popular culture or government efforts, the United States government in particular, to eradicate wolves.

Regardless, the ultimate argument of this book remains the same and perfectly – if not even more – relevant.

Contents

Introduction

For tens of thousands of years, even before recorded history, humanity believed in the werewolf: a being that could transform between human and wolf. The concept of lycanthropy is deeply ingrained in the human mind: the duality of man[2] and beast and of civilization and savagery. While the dual nature of lycanthropy and its relation to mankind – whether one believes in monsters or not – presents an entire subject in itself, as do the many other facets of the werewolf that could be explored in fiction today but generally are not, contemplating the werewolf also prompts an important question: is the legendary werewolf good or evil? Such a question has been asked and answered many times throughout both historical legends and fiction, with the responders ranging from historians and theologians to modern fiction

---

[2] In this study, all instances of "man," "men," and "mankind" refer, unless specified literally or contextually, to *humans* and *humanity*, including both men and women. Similarly, this study uses male pronouns when speaking of werewolves generally; this is not meant to imply that there are no female werewolves. There absolutely were multiple werewolf women in assorted legends around the globe.

writers and occultists, and while the answers have varied over time, the generally accepted answer today is simple: werewolves are malevolent.

Although there are many other questions that could be asked regarding werewolves, one pressing question is: what does one mean by "malevolent?" Are all werewolves this way, according to both those who believed they exist and those who write about them in fiction? Is a person who is cursed to become a werewolf doomed to become evil also, even if they were once good? Does this change affect both the human and the animal form? These questions have been debated as well, and depending upon the source, a werewolf may not necessarily have been a bad person, but they will carry out inhuman acts of savagery, violence, and – more often than not – cannibalism while in their wolfish form. The idea of a werewolf as an insane being is one deeply ingrained in cultural history, and this idea has been welcomed into popular culture to the point that, today, finding a werewolf committing an act of benevolence is almost seen as comical, considered as preposterous as believing in werewolves themselves. In fact, the fairly modern term "clinical lycanthropy" refers to a specific mental disease, in which one imagines that they are transforming into a wolf.[3] Thus, long have werewolves been associated with madmen – at least since the Early Modern period, around the time when the terms "lycanthropia" and "lycanthropus" were first invented.[4]

In addition to associations with insanity, werewolves are frequently equated to evil itself: malevolence, rather than just animalistic behavior. The average consumer of popular culture thinks of werewolves as being not only violent beasts, but also evil monsters, often associated with demons. Such connections spring from many different roots, including how the wolf animal itself has always been cast as a villain – a fate that the werewolf has also shared for quite some time, and it is

---

[3] Garlipp 19

[4] These words, which eventually became "lycanthropy" and "lycanthrope," the latter of which has recently suffered nonsensical mutilation into "lycan" in modern culture, were first used by Reginald Scot in 1584 (Otten 8), derived from Greek "lykanthropos." Just as "werewolf" literally means "man-wolf," "lycanthrope" means "wolf-man." The term "werewolf" was first used in English much earlier, as will be discussed later in this study.

a fate most undeserved.

Unfortunately, society refuses to release both werewolves and wolves from such stigmas: they remain malevolent beings, or at least troublemakers and undesirables, with their better qualities cast into the background in favor of the images of ferocity, gluttony, violence, thievery, and evil that have been imposed upon them across cultural history. How did this idea of werewolves become so deeply ingrained into popular culture? What gave rise to the concept of werewolves at all, and why are they portrayed so negatively today? Which depictions are the ones that fiction writers today usually reference – and are these depictions based on any kind of legend? Were werewolves, in fact, ever seen in a *positive* light, or at least a more sympathetic one than the maddened, terrifying beast – or walking dog joke – depicted now? A thorough study of history reveals many of the answers.

Thus, this study will begin by examining the original werewolf legends and the natures of the werewolves therein – in particular, their morality – throughout history,[5] leading up

---

[5] It should be noted that, though werewolves are a worldwide

to present day distortions of these old myths, and then ultimately it will present how benevolent portrayals of werewolves could benefit society as a whole, including improvements upon storytelling, education, and lessening of the unwarranted hatred and fear with which wolves have been viewed for millennia: a hatred that has become so ingrained into the average person that their immediate reaction upon seeing a wolf is a negative one, often based in fear, though they may not entirely realize why. The first chapter of this book, "The Ancients and Werewolves," will explain the very earliest legends in werewolf history, such as those in prehistory, as well as the ancient Greek and Roman concepts of lycanthropy, which still influence werewolf perceptions today. The second chapter, "Werewolves of the Middle Ages," will discuss the many ways in which werewolves were seen and portrayed throughout the Middle Ages, ranging from Scandinavian tales

---

phenomenon of mythology, this study will not extensively explore legends from some regions, such as Asia. This is due to European legends forming the primary basis for the majority of modern werewolf concepts in media, not to belittle any of the many fascinating worldwide werewolf mythologies that I will likely compile and discuss in a later publication.

to medieval romances such as Marie de France's *Bisclavret* – which are very different from most modern concepts of werewolves based in the medieval period, as seen throughout many films and video games. "Chapter III – Werewolves Go Mad: The Transition into Modernity," will highlight the contrasting depictions of werewolves in the Middle Ages to werewolves in the Early Modern Period, transitioning into what is common today, with a particular focus upon the rise of the modern conception of werewolves as madmen, symbols of insanity, and servants or spawn of the Devil, a combination brought about by the rise of scientific thought, greater law and civilization, and religion, all of which were inexorably tied together at that time. "Chapter IV – The Moon Waxes: The Werewolf Popularity Surge," will extensively examine and discuss the recent resurgence of werewolf popularity, such as the earliest werewolf films, the werewolf films of the 1980s and how they tragically aided in urging audiences to view werewolves as comical, and the *Twilight* series, which, for better or for worse, brought werewolves into a more popular light than ever before; this chapter will, of course, also include the single most pivotal point in the creation of the werewolf concept ingrained so deeply in society today: the 1941 film *The Wolf Man*. The final chapter of this study, "The Benefits of Reintroducing the Benevolent Werewolf," as well as the epilogue, "Turning the Tables," will discuss how depicting the legendary werewolf as a benevolent being could, potentially, benefit society as a whole.

If popular culture began exploring werewolves as benevolent beings, then not only would this view provide much-needed variety among werewolf stories and possibly encourage writers to perform primary research regarding these legendary creatures, but also it would introduce to modern society the idea that the wolf itself is, as an animal, not an evil monster to be hunted and feared. By depicting the lycanthrope as benevolent, society could return the werewolf to its ancient status as a symbol of morality and a means through which stories explore the nature of humans and animals, as well as concepts of wilderness and civilization, among many other themes. Likewise, the return of the benevolent werewolf might achieve still more important goals. It might, to begin with, improve storytelling by providing more thematic depth and moral exploration, particularly in terms of human "versus" animal – and whether there is, or should ever be, this idea of "versus" between these two entities. In addition, portrayals of benevolent werewolves could aid in creating recognition that werewolf legends have a rich and varied history in nearly every culture in the world, thus providing an argument against the modern idea of the werewolf as a simplistic monster with no complexity or meaning. Finally, negative portrayals of werewolves also influence society's conception of wolves, which are, themselves, depicted in an unfairly negative manner, and have been for many ages. It is a conception that is rooted in primal hatred and fear, and these negative views of wolves result in humanity committing great cruelty, harm, and slaughter to wolves today and throughout all recent history.

The purposes of this study, then, are to provide context for the werewolf legend and its status in modern culture, to examine the werewolf legend throughout history, and, ultimately, to argue that portraying werewolves in a positive and serious light could aid in creating more meaningful and thought-provoking stories and possibly lending the concept of the werewolf at least some of the respect it once had, in bringing about a realization that the werewolf legend is a truly ancient concept that exists across multiple cultures, and finally in fostering a more positive understanding of the wolf as an animal. After all, if a malevolent werewolf is a creature who is both man and wolf, society is not only condemning wolves, the animals from which we receive so much, including our precious domesticated dogs – it is also condemning man's own nature and willpower.

THE WEREWOLF: PAST AND FUTURE

Chapter I – The Ancients and Werewolves

In order to understand the means through which werewolves came to be seen as simplistic, malevolent monsters by modern society, and why this is a historically inaccurate and ignorant depiction (at least, in terms of the history of legends), one must first be made aware of the earliest origins of the werewolf myth. Werewolf legends were told by many societies throughout time, even before recorded history; indeed, scholars argue over what represents the "first werewolf," in part because there is no real way of knowing the age of the werewolf legend – particularly since, like many legends, a great deal of werewolf stories were only retold orally. Ranging from the earliest humans and even pre-humans to the Greeks and Romans, the werewolf in ancient times takes many shapes across multiple cultures, spanning, essentially, the entire world, and certainly the entire historical range of wolves. Among perhaps the most important of all werewolf legends, and some of the earliest to be recorded, were the ones told by the ancient Greeks. The belief in werewolves was, naturally, then carried over into ancient Rome, but the werewolf also independently arose in other cultures around the world, including but not limited to Europe, North America, and Asia. However, the belief in werewolves may have existed as early as the Paleolithic Age, around 45,000 BP.[6]

One might wonder exactly what led the earliest humans to believe in animal transformation, even causing some to revere the ability, but these beliefs are now largely irrelevant to popular culture today. Although there have been many changes in society since the days of shamanistic hunter-gatherers, werewolf legends may have had their roots in such cultures. Matthew Beresford makes plain in *The White Devil: The Werewolf in European Culture* that the idea of a person turning into a wolf most likely arose in Europe because shape-shifting legends generally take the form of the animal a society fears the most.[7] While this is clearly true, werewolves also appear in nearly every culture on earth that had wolves at any given point

---

[6] Beresford 19; the year is given by Beresford as BP (Before Present), due to the carbon dating process of prehistoric artifacts.

[7] Beresford 19-20

in history, rather than just Europe,[8] and those depictions were not always necessarily undertaken because society "feared" the wolf in a negative way. Indeed, although other shape-shifter legends certainly existed across various cultures, werewolves boast the widest range and the longest-lasting impact across multiple societies through time.[9]

In terms of prehistoric European cultures, the idea of men transforming into wolves was often portrayed in a positive light, given that early humans revered predators for their ability to hunt prey. Likewise, humans wore wolf skins on their backs when going on a hunt, so that they might better blend in with their surroundings and also gain the then-coveted power of the wolf; they may have also believed themselves to be shape-shifting into them.[10] Early man domesticated wolves, as the theory goes, so that they eventually

---

[8] Douglas 25; "Evidence of belief in the werewolf legend is found throughout the whole range of the wolf's former habitat: from the northern tundra of Europe and Asia down to the shores of the Mediterranean, as far east as India and China, and throughout North America in the west."

[9] All of these instances refer to the time frames previously provided by Beresford, dating as far back as 45,000 BP.

[10] Beresford 23-24

became the assorted breeds of domestic dogs so loved today. Since wolves and men cultivated that unique relationship, humans felt a kinship with wolves that they did not share with other predators that they were unable to domesticate.[11] Overall, the earliest werewolf legends, according to some scholars, may have sprung from the domestication of wolves. However, a stronger argument focuses on early man's conception of wolves as the ultimate predator in whom they still saw many social bonds and other similarities to humans: emotions, reverence for the dead, and many more. Early societies craved to have the hunting prowess of a wolf pack, leading them to create strange rituals, including the wearing of wolf skins in order to harness some of their power, as well as using wolfdogs to hunt.

Perhaps the most important trait carried over from the werewolf legends of early man may be the idea that werewolves

---

[11] Beresford 24. Beresford's theory regarding animal domestication certainly carries some weight, but it does not take into account that werewolves are far from "domesticated" in their myths, nor do the themes of werewolf legends, or other shape-shifter legends, involve such elements.

transform when the moon is full, at least according to Adam Douglas, author of *The Beast Within: A History of the Werewolf.*[12] Douglas claims that the full moon's association with werewolves also predates recorded history,[13] in that the full moon became a symbol of the hunt. Although Douglas provides many reasons for the full moon being associated with hunting, including the simple fact that wolves howl more often during a full moon,[14] he does not draw much attention to the fact that the full moon has long been thought to change human and animal thought patterns, nor does he directly mention how these ideas of the moon and hunting lead him to postulate that a werewolf transforming during this time originated in the

---

[12] Douglas 46-47

[13] To be precise, Douglas claims this "unarguably" originated in the prehistoric period, though he provides primarily conjecture and strange guesswork, all of which seem generally unrelated to the actual act of a man (supposedly) transforming into a wolf, as appears in later werewolf legends and in the Hollywood films mentioned by Douglas himself.

[14] Douglas seems intent on mentioning just about every conceivable reason why the full moon could be a symbol of the hunt, except for the fact that the moon provides humans more light by which to see (and he makes no mention of the various scientifically proven psychological influences of the full moon).

prehistoric era.

Thus, werewolves – or wolves, or hunters wearing wolf-skins who sought the power of the wolf – were often seen in a positive light in prehistory. They were, at the very least, respected and revered for their keen hunting prowess. Naturally, society's views on wolves and their supernatural relations changed over time, particularly following the beginning of recorded history, just as more precise ideas of actual werewolves themselves – meaning people who physically transform into wolves, rather than just early humans in wolf skins hunting by the light of the full moon – came into the minds of men. It remains important to note, of course, that we cannot know with certainty that prehistoric hunters did not hold concepts of themselves as transforming merely because we, as outsiders eons later, see them only as people in wolf skins.

One may ask, then, who or what was the "first werewolf?" To claim that one can trace werewolf legends – many of which predate recorded history – back to the "first" one is surely a combination of arrogance and ignorance, but, today, it has become a popular notion to assert that King Lycaon, from Greek mythology, was the "first" werewolf.[15] Other scholars, such as Adam Douglas, claim there are other "first" werewolves; Douglas states that Ishtar causing the transformation of a shepherd into a wolf in *The Epic of Gilgamesh*, written around 2750 BC, is the first recorded instance of a human's transforming into a wolf – though that does not necessarily denote "werewolf."[16] Defining the "first werewolf" depends

---

[15] The *Teen Wolf* MTV TV series, for example, conveys its own werewolf history and lore, stating that Lycaon was the first werewolf, and that the curse originated with him. Other stories, such as the novel *Hunted* by Nick Stead, follow this example, whether independently or not.

[16] Douglas 48. However, counting this instance from the *Epic of Gilgamesh* as "the first werewolf" is an odd statement. Yes, the shepherd is turned into a wolf, which is the same as many other werewolf legends (even Lycaon's), but the choice of turning him into a wolf seems insignificant in terms of meaning. The fact that Lycaon's transformation was intended as meaningful lends more power to the idea that King Lycaon may be the earliest recorded instance of a werewolf legend, since his actions led him to be specifically turned into a *wolf*, rather than into some other creature. The shepherd in *Gilgamesh* is only turned into a wolf so that his dogs will attack him, and other animals are substituted in later tales of this exact same type (such as Artemis turning a mortal into a deer so his dogs will rip him apart in a later Greek myth), making the choice of a wolf in the *Epic of Gilgamesh* feel arbitrary enough that it seems almost unfair to give it such importance in the history of werewolf mythology.

largely upon how exactly one wants to define a "werewolf," along with a willingness to acknowledge that records of whichever legend *truly* told of the "first werewolf" could not possibly exist. For the purpose of this study, a werewolf means – quite simply – a man who undergoes a physical transformation, voluntary or involuntary, into specifically a wolf. Therefore, it is important to start with the popular favorite "first werewolf:" King Lycaon of Arcadia.

The Greek king named Lycaon ruled over the region of Arcadia, which is often considered a pastoral paradise, at least in Early Modern culture. Although most scholars refer to the version of this tale as retold in Ovid's *Metamorphoses*, many variants of Lycaon's story exist, one of which – told by the Greek poet, commentator, and grammarian Lycophron – says that Lycaon, as well as all his sons, and even all the other people of Arcadia were turned into wolves. Ovid, however, tells a different tale: Lycaon doubts the divinity of Zeus when the god visits Arcadia. In order to test Zeus's divinity, Lycaon attempts to feed him cooked human flesh and have him assassinated in the night. When Zeus realizes what Lycaon is doing, Lycaon tries to flee in fear. But as he runs into the fields of Arcadia, Lycaon is transformed into a wolf.[17] Lycaon thus represents not only one of the first werewolves, but also one of the few werewolves to have a transformation sequence of sorts, as well as an early example of an involuntary transformation with negative connotations. Not only is Lycaon transformed into a wolf, but his change seems to be permanent, unlike the transformations in many of the later tales of Arcadian werewolves.

Although King Lycaon is usually the first legend to spring to mind in terms of werewolves in ancient Greece, many

---

[17] Ovid 8. Ovid's description of Lycaon's transformation further solidifies the idea that Lycaon was the first werewolf, particularly in the traditional sense, as werewolves in popular culture now feel incomplete without a terrifying transformation. Ovid says, "[Lycaon] howled his heart out, trying in vain to speak. / With rabid mouth he turned his lust for slaughter / Against the flocks, delighting still in blood. / His clothes changed to coarse hair, his arms to legs— / He was a wolf, yet kept some human trace, / the same grey hair, the same fierce face, the same / Wild eyes, the same image of savagery." Other translations of Ovid take a more or less visceral stance when describing the change. Indeed, later werewolf legends do not mimic Lycaon's tale in terms of detailing the werewolf's transformation from man into beast, providing yet another way in which the legend of King Lycaon remains one of the most influential and important werewolf stories from a historical standpoint.

other tales also existed, as told by Greek and Roman authors such as Virgil, Herodotus, Pliny, Petronius, and many others, including Pomponius Mela and Agriopas.[18] Consistent among many ancient Greek accounts is the idea that the people of Arcadia, since the cursing of King Lycaon, adopted werewolf rituals into their very culture. Other werewolf tales vary a bit more wildly, with some werewolves undergoing a voluntary transformation as opposed to an involuntary one. Others retain the ability to transform back and forth as they please, while some must remain in their wolf form for a particular amount of time before they resume a human shape, and some will not become a wolf again unless once more engaging in the same ritual.

In *The Book of Were-Wolves*, noted werewolf scholar Sabine Baring-Gould gives a concise list of almost every ancient Greek and Roman mention of werewolves, and from his citations, other scholars have discussed these instances in further detail. One such example appears in the writings of Herodotus, who says that the Neuri people are "sorcerers, if one

---

[18] Baring-Gould, *Book 9-10*

is to believe the Scythians and the Greeks established in Scythia."[19] He further states that, once a year, the Neurians transform themselves into wolves, and they maintain this form for several days before returning to their human shape. Herodotus, however, does not provide any details regarding exactly why they do this, nor does he give any details about their behavior. Pomponius Mela also states that the Neurians undergo willing transformations to and from the form of a wolf, though he does not provide the same level of specificity as does Herodotus.[20]

Multiple sources describe various strange werewolf rituals in ancient Greece, particularly in Arcadia, the region

---

[19] Baring-Gould, *Book* 9. Herodotus referring to the Neurians as "sorcerers," as opposed to simply "werewolves" serves to highlight that not all cases of wolf transformation were specifically categorized as "lycanthropy," particularly during this time period. Similarly, many creatures and myths in folklore are not so sharply categorized as researchers – or even fiction writers – would prefer for them to be today. This shall become very important in Chapter III, in which it will be highlighted that the line meant to exist between "werewolves" and "sorcerers" in legend has been blurred by werewolf scholars, and this has had incredible impact upon the modern day negative image of the werewolf.

[20] Baring-Gould, *Book* 9

ruled, at one point, by King Lycaon. For instance, Pliny cites Evanthes as discussing a festival, "Jupiter Lycaeus," named after the Arcadian portrayal of Zeus, in which a member of the Antaeus family was selected by drawing lots. The chosen one was brought to a lake in Arcadia, where he hung his clothes on a tree, swam across the river, and exited the other side as a wolf. The story says that if he did not eat human flesh for the nine years he spent in his wolf form, he could swim back across the lake and return to his human form.[21] Agriopas writes that Demaenatus, a contender in the Olympic games, once partook in an Arcadian ritual also related to Jupiter Lycaus, during which he ate human flesh. As a result, he immediately transformed into a wolf and remained that way for ten years. When he returned to his human shape, he then went on to participate in the Olympics.[22]

Also referencing werewolf legends in Arcadia, Montague Summers in *Werewolf* – as cited elsewhere by other sources – quotes extensively from the eighth book of

---

[21] Baring-Gould, *Book* 9-10
[22] Baring-Gould, *Book* 10

Pausanias's *Description of Greece*, in which Pausanias lengthily describes werewolf rituals and legends in Arcadia.[23] Among these descriptions are mentions of a son of Lycaon, Pelasgus, building a city named Lycosura on Mount Lycaeus: which is often known today as Mount Lykaion. The Arcadians referred to Zeus as "Zeus Lycaean," or as the Romans later described him in writings about the same portrayal, "Jupiter Lyaeus." Pelasgus also founded the Lucaean games, similar to the Olympics, all named after his father, Lycaon, and involving sacrifices to their Lycaean Zeus, who transformed his faithful servants into wolves following the completion of their sacrifice ritual. Pausanias, however, makes note that he does not believe in the wolf transformation, saying that he thinks it nothing but a story, although "it has been handed down among the Arcadians from antiquity, and probably in its favor... They say that from the time of Lycaon downwards a man has always been turned into a wolf at the sacrifice of Lycaean Zeus."[24] It is, yet again, important to note that this transformation is

---

[23] Summers, *Werewolf* 134-135

[24] Summers, *Werewolf* 134

different than the transformation of King Lycaon: it was never permanent, and after nine years of not eating human flesh, the werewolf returned to their human form.

Another werewolf tale from this time period endures in *The Satyricon,* by Petronius: the oft-cited tale told by Niceros.[25] The story is a simple one, though it displays many stranger aspects later adopted by other werewolf legends, particularly others in the same region. In his story, Niceros stays with a host whom Niceros asks to accompany him on evening walks. One night, when "[t]he Moon shone bright as day,"[26] they stop around a "Burying-place,"[27] where the host pauses to gaze at the stars.[28] When next Niceros looks at his

---

[25] Much like the story of King Lycaon, Niceros's tale is cited and discussed by nearly every werewolf scholar through history, including two of the most influential: Baring-Gould and Summers.

[26] Petronius 231. This line implies that the transformation may have been connected, at least somewhat, with the moonlight and/or a full moon.

[27] Petronius 231. The fact that this event takes place in a graveyard bears great similarity to later werewolf tales, particularly beliefs regarding werewolves as madmen in the Early Modern period.

[28] Alternatively, the host could be gazing at the moon before his transformation. The text specifies "star-gazing," but depending upon one's outlook, this could easily be taken to indicate the influence of

host, he sees him nude, having shed his clothes by the side of the road. The host then urinates around his clothing and transforms into a wolf, running away with a howl. For whatever reason, and perhaps due to some form of comic irony from Petronius, Niceros feels the need to punctuate his story with the reminder of this event's reality, implying the possibility of some disbelief or at least skepticism in transformation legends at the time, saying, "Don't think I jest, for I value no Man's Estate at that rate, as well to tell a Lye."[29] Niceros approaches the host's clothes, which have now turned to stone. When Niceros returns to his lover at the house in which he is staying, she tells him about a wolf who slaughtered many cattle before a servant managed to wound it in the neck. Shocked, Niceros returns immediately to the clothes that had turned to stone, but he finds that they are gone, replaced by a pool of blood. Coming home again, Niceros discovers his host in bed with a dressed wound in his neck. Niceros ends his story by saying, "I understood afterwards that he was a Fellow that

---

the moon, or at least the night, on the host turning into a werewolf.
[29] Petronius 233

could change his Skin, but from that day forward, could never eat a bit of Bread with him, no if you'd have kill'd me."[30]

Niceros's story displays many aspects important to werewolf tales, as mentioned by Leslie A. Sconduto in her book *Metamorphoses of the Werewolf,*[31] as well as other scholars, such as Douglas in *The Beast Within.*[32] Niceros emphasizes how afraid he is of the werewolf and his transformation: something often exhibited in werewolf fiction today. Likewise, as Sconduto and Douglas also emphasize, Niceros's tale includes a motif that becomes very important in later werewolf stories in that the werewolf, in human form, carries wounds that others inflicted upon his wolf form. Douglas also notes the moonlight in the scene,[33] although he notes primarily that Niceros needed the

---

[30] Petronius 233

[31] Sconduto 9-12. It should be noted, however, that Sconduto herself makes clear that her study is not meant to be a history of werewolves (as she says on page 7, "It is of course not the purpose of this study to trace the history of the werewolf through its metamorphoses in modern films."), though she includes much werewolf history, anyway, and studies thereof.

[32] Douglas 51-53

[33] Douglas 52

moonlight to see the transformation and that the moon shone brightly, without speculating whether or not there existed some connection between the moonlight and the transformation. Thus, although it exhibits many of the more unusual aspects of werewolf transformations that were not carried over into modern popular culture, Niceros's tale forms a very important early werewolf legend.

One small detail, overlooked by a few scholars, is that Petronius uses the term *"versipellis"*[34] to describe the werewolf, rather than the term "werewolf" itself. The Latin word versipellis means "turn-coat" or "turn-skin,"[35] implying a sort of shapeshifter. However, when using it again in his own works, Pliny specifically notes that this word is used to describe various Arcadian rituals and other beliefs of men turning into wolves, hinting that "versipellis" may simply be another word from antiquity for "werewolf," much like other terms discussed in later chapters. Pliny writes of the legends with great skepticism, unlike his contemporaries, saying that they are

[34] Baring-Gould, *Book* 10
[35] Summers, *Werewolf* 138

"meere fabulous untruths."[36] Of course, in either case, he is unsure enough of his skepticism to cite numerous examples of werewolves in Greece, nonetheless.

Plato, Homer, and Virgil allude to werewolves as well, completing a large set of Greek and Roman writers who mention the legendary beasts. In book eight of Plato's *Republic*, he alludes to the werewolf rituals in Arcadia,[37] doing so in a sufficiently neutral manner that he does not reveal a stance on whether he believes in such legends, instead only stating that he has heard of the rituals and transformations. Homer refers to an entire race called the Lycians, who worshiped the god Lycegenaean Apollo, meaning "born of the wolf."[38] When Leto transformed herself as a wolf, she descended into the land of the Hyperboreans, calling that region Lycia: "of a wolf." Apollo also went to Lycia in the form of a wolf. Although the Lycians may not transform into wolves as specifically as the Arcadians did through their sacrifices to Zeus, given a lack of further

---

[36] Summers, *Werewolf* 138

[37] Summers, *Werewolf* 142

[38] Beresford 46

history regarding them (provided by Homer or any other source), we cannot be sure of what beliefs and rituals they may have had, and in either case, the gods they revered both transformed into wolves, themselves. Virgil also mentions werewolf transformations, though it seems scholars often take less interest in general with his tale, for whatever reason.[39] In his eighth *eclogue*, around 37 BC, Virgil includes a character called Moeris, who "turn[s] [into a] wolf and hide[s] in the woods."[40] Instead of undergoing cannibalistic rituals, being cursed by a god, or willfully taking the wolf form through some other unknown means, Moeris apparently can adopt this shape using alchemy. There seems to be no negative stigma attached to his transformation into a wolf, and Moeris can clearly change back whenever he pleases, as he willingly turns into a wolf to "hide" from others, very much unlike many werewolves found in popular culture today.

Despite what many consumers of popular culture may

---

[39] Not many sources include Virgil's mention of wolf transformation, except for Baring-Gould's *Book of Were-Wolves* on page 9, who quotes the source in its original Latin, providing no translation or further discussion, and Sconduto on pages 8-9.

[40] Sconduto 8

believe, many of the most important werewolf legends originated in antiquity, rather than the Middle Ages. Although the very first werewolf legends originated well before recorded history, the Greeks and Romans told tales of werewolves that truly began the tradition still carried on today in popular culture, though they varied far more regarding the werewolf's transformation, nature, and morality than does much of today's fiction. Other civilizations across the world had legends of werewolves, each independently conceptualized, with particularly influential tales originating in the regions of Scandinavia and North America, while others exist across Asia and particularly in China.[41] However, it is the stories from the Middle Ages that provide the most interesting and strange variety of werewolf appearances, personalities, and abilities,

---

[41] As Sabine Baring-Gould so expertly phrases it on page 11 of *The Book of Were-Wolves*, "Half the world believes, or believed in, were-wolves, and they were supposed to haunt the Norwegian forests by those who had never remotely been connected with Arcadia [the primary seat of many Greek werewolf legends that survived history]: and the superstition had probably struck deep its roots into the Scandinavian and Teutonic minds, ages before Lycaon existed; and we have only to glance at Oriental literature, to see it as firmly engrafted in the imaginations of the Easterners."

rather than the very oldest of tales – and it is these medieval legends that form a primary focus of this study, given medieval tales often depict werewolves far more sympathetically than do the cursed werewolves of antiquity.

THE WEREWOLF: PAST AND FUTURE

Chapter II – Werewolves of the Middle Ages

The Middle Ages arguably represent the most important time period in the history of the werewolf legend; if for no other reason, one could consider this period important to werewolves because of its influences on the modern idea that the werewolf is a medieval creature (even if such modern depictions seem incredibly unaware of the *actual* werewolf tales from the Middle Ages). Although the idea of werewolves certainly originated before the medieval period, and several concepts that have maintained their hold in popular culture today did not even originate in medieval tales, werewolves have nonetheless become closely tied to the Middle Ages, particularly in fantasy fiction. Werewolves continued to run rampant in stories all across the world during the Middle Ages, including most prominently Europe and Scandinavia, from which have been recovered many assorted werewolf tales: some that people believed to be true, others that they (most likely) knew to be fiction. Werewolves in the legends of the Middle Ages vary wildly in terms of appearance, nature, personality, and abilities – including some of the most morally just and sympathetic werewolves to ever appear in any kind of story, such as portrayed in Marie de France's *Bisclavret*. Given how many werewolf legends arose in the Middle Ages, however, there are far too many to include, particularly in detail, in a study such as this one. Therefore, the focus of this chapter will be to convey an understanding of the rich detail and thought-provoking themes of the varied medieval werewolf tales, as well as detailing those most pertinent to this study of the morality and nature of werewolves in legend and popular culture.

In Scandinavia, werewolf traditions appear across all forms of literature, though they appear perhaps most notably in multiple sagas and in the legends of the berserkers or ulfheðnir. So many tales are there of animal shape-shifting in Scandinavian legend that one could dedicate an entire essay or even a book to these alone, including men turning into wolves, bears, boars, and more.[42] Werewolves were particularly

---

[42] Baring-Gould, *Book* 12-18. Shape-shifters were so common in Scandinavian lore, in fact, that they had many names to refer to such

common, given the natural wolves in the region and their, presumably, relatively frequent interactions with humans. Interestingly, in old Norse tales, the methods one had to use to become a werewolf – or any manner of shape-shifter – varied much more wildly than in popular culture today, including wearing a magical skin, the soul departing the human body and entering the shape of an animal, and lastly, chanting an incantation to assume an illusionary animal form, though the latter two examples did not result in "true" shape-shifting.[43] Perhaps the most well-known werewolfish incident in a Norse saga occurs in the *Völsunga Saga*, when Sigmund and Sinfjötli find two sleeping men with wolf skins hanging in their house, and upon donning the skins, Sigmund and Sinfjötli transform

---

individuals. For instance, they called them *eigi einhamir*, or "not of one skin." They were said to change from one body to another, and when they shifted, they assumed the nature of the creature in question. Such individuals were extremely strong, and those imbued with their own strength as well as their animal form's power were called *hamrammr*. Some *eigi einhamir* could assume wolf forms, but they were not restricted solely to wolves, which is why they are not discussed in more detail in this study. However, it is important to note that these shape-shifters not only increased their strength, but they maintained their intelligence regardless of their form.

[43] Baring-Gould, *Book* 12

into wolves and cannot change back. Although they are said to assume a wolf's nature, they still seem capable of speaking to each other, as they make an agreement that they will each test their strength against seven men, and they are to howl if they get into trouble. Ultimately, they kill seven men and then Sigmund kills eleven alone, after which Sigmund and Sinfjötli get into an argument and later shed their wolf forms and curse them, with Sigmund blaming the wolf forms for their argument.[44]

An important and interesting element in Scandinavian werewolf legends is the berserkers, or ulfheðnir, warriors who went into battle wearing the skins of wolves or sometimes other animals.[45] The ulfheðnir are mentioned in a few sagas,

---

[44] Baring-Gould, *Book* 13

[45] For years, scholars (including Baring-Gould himself, who makes mention of it in *The Book of Were-Wolves*) have debated the meaning and origin of the word "berserker." Some say it comes from words meaning "bare of shirt," and others say it means "bear-shirt," implying that they wear bear skins. In my own research, however, and from asking individuals who both read and study Old Norse, I have personally found that the idea of "berserker" implying these warriors wore *no* shirt, as stated by the irreplaceable Snorri Sturluson, is far more accurate than the idea that they are "bear-warriors," given both the etymology of "berserker" and the fact that nearly all of our

such as the *Vatnsdæla Saga*, in which they are described as "Those berserkir who were called *ulfheðnir*, had got wolf-skins over their mail coats."[46] In the *Holmverja Saga*, one character is described as being "son of *Ulfheðin*, wolfskin coat, son of *Ulfhamr*, wolf-shaped, son of *Ulf*, wolf, son of *Ulfhamr*, wolf-shaped, who could change forms."[47] According to legend, berserkers were warriors who had the ability to fly into a superhuman rage and gain the might of an animal, and as a result, they were feared warriors all across Scandinavia. Berserkers supposedly could endure impossible amounts of pain and perform inhuman feats of strength when they entered into their enraged – or berserk – state, in which they

---

surviving depictions and mentions of berserkers in writing and imagery shows them wearing wolf skins, like the ulfheðnir (who are generally mentioned when berserkers are, or sometimes without any mention of the word "berserker" at all). There were occasional mentions of bear warriors as well, and certainly bear transformations in Scandinavian folklore, but these were not generally associated with berserkers. Berserkers overall seem more closely connected to wolves than bears, and in one instance even boars, and their etymology does not seem to imply any specific connection to bears, either.

[46] Baring-Gould, *Book* 19

[47] Baring-Gould, *Book* 19

behaved like maddened animals: "Their eyes glared as though a flame burned in their sockets, they ground their teeth, and frothed at the mouth; they gnawed at their shield rims, and are said to have sometimes bitten them through, and as they rushed into conflict they ... howled as wolves."[48]

Numerous more examples of werewolves and werewolf-like figures, including other berserkers, appear throughout Norse sagas and other accounts. For instance, a man named Ulf – meaning wolf – went on Viking expeditions, and he was an intelligent man whom others often sought for advice. As the day ended, however, at dusk, "he became so savage that few dared exchange a word with him ... People said that he was much given to changing form, so he was called the evening-wolf, *kveldúlfr*."[49] Baring-Gould also mentions other werewolves in Scandinavia, saying, "It is said of these men in the engagement who were were-wolves, or those on whom came the berserkr rage, that as long as the fit was on them no

---

[48] Baring-Gould, *Book* 21, quoted from a Roman account. Note the specificity to wolves.

[49] Baring-Gould, *Book* 22, quoted from the *Aigla*

one could oppose them, they were so strong."[50]

Although the fact is not specifically related to
werewolves, it is noteworthy that the Norse had a double
meaning for the word for wolf, *vargr*, and this may have further
aided in casting werewolves in a negative light in later ages.
According to Baring-Gould, "*Vargr* is the same as *u-argr*,
restless; *argr* being the same as Anglo-Saxon *earg*. *Vargr* ...
signified a wolf, and also a godless man."[51] Baring-Gould even
quotes a legal sentence as saying, "[H]e shall be driven away as
a wolf, and chased so far as men chase wolves farthest."[52] The
etymology of the various terms for werewolf can potentially
come into question here, as Baring-Gould spends time
breaking down words such as *werewolf* (English for werewolf,
from Old English "man-wolf"), *loup-garou* (French for
werewolf), *varulf* (Danish), *vaira-ulf* (Gothic), and others,
searching for connections between these words and the Norse
term for an outlaw, in an attempt to discover whether *vargr* as
a word for "outlaw" bears any connection with the negative

---

[50] Baring-Gould, *Book* 23

[51] Baring-Gould, *Book* 24

[52] Baring-Gould, *Book* 24

portrayal of werewolves.[53] Ultimately, such negativity most likely stemmed more from later era Christianity and its connection with law and concepts of wilderness versus civilization, the Early Modern period, and the rise of scientific reasoning behind all thought, which will soon be discussed.

However, not all werewolves in Scandinavia were seen as being directly connected to a violent nature or to criminals; in fact, the region hosts a wide variety of werewolf legends, and the Scandinavian cultural view of wolves was not as overtly negative as the viewpoint of many other Europeans. Although wolves were also seen as tricksters and scavengers of the battlefield,[54] and some wolves were giant monsters, such as the great wolf Fenrir, wolves were nonetheless sacred animals of the ancient Norse god Odin.[55] As Beresford mentions, Odin

---

[53] Baring-Gould, *Book* 24

[54] This is why, in some tales, valkyries were said to ride giant wolves. As the "choosers of the slain" (as valkyries were often called) were said to appear on abandoned battlefields, valkyries were associated with the animals people often saw looking among the dead: wolves, ravens, and other kinds of birds.

[55] Odin himself has now found a means to enter broader popular culture through the Marvel *Thor* movies, although his legendary wolves do not appear in those films, and the films distort him (and

created the first wolves, Geri and Freki, to provide himself with companions in the loneliness of his wanderings. Because Odin wandered everywhere, and his wolves followed him, wolves spread all across the world, and "[t]he way the wolves celebrated life filled Odin with joy."[56] According to legend, when Odin created the first humans, he told them to look to wolves for instruction: "The wolf could teach them how to care for their family, how to cooperate with each other in the hunt for food, and how to protect and defend their families."[57] A final quotation from this same tale regarding Odin solidifies the fact that wolves were seen as a positive force: "The wolf gave much wisdom and skill to the early humans. In the old times the wolf was respected. 'To be Wolf Clan (*Ulfhednar*) was a great honor. A Wolf Brother.'"[58] However, as the Vikings converted to Christianity near the end of the tenth century, their view of wolves and werewolves changed: "No longer was it accepted

---

Norse mythology in general) in other ways.

[56] Beresford 79

[57] Beresford 79

[58] Beresford 79

practice for a man to aspire to take the wolf's form."[59]

Much like what happened with the Vikings, as the medieval world converted to Christianity and began to view the concept of wilderness as an enemy, werewolves were cast in a steadily more negative light. The king of England from 1016-1035, King Cnut, issued the *Ecclesiastical Ordinances XXVI*, in which he specifically mentions the werewolf in relation to the Devil, saying, "[be watchful, that] the madly audacious werewolf do not too widely devastate, nor bite too many of the spiritual flock."[60] This passage marks one of the earliest instances in which the term "werewolf" is virtually equated to the Devil or demons in general in Christianity, which becomes relatively common in later medieval writings – and it also marks the first recorded use of the word "werewolf." Christianity, however, as will be discussed later, does not solely participate in negative portrayals of werewolves or wolves and in fact fostered some positive views of them. Regardless,

---

[59] Beresford 80

[60] Beresford 80, quoting *Ecclesiastical Ordinances XXVI* by King Cnut of England

instead of the wolf being a brother and wolf transformations being desirable, or at least not worthy of condemnation, Christianity and science – with the rise of larger civilizations pushing back against wilderness and the very concept of it – largely altered the view of werewolves, turning them into demonic creatures associated with evil and witchcraft, who romp across the countryside leaving death and destruction in their wake. As stated by Beresford, "[T]he use of the werewolf as a religious scapegoat by the Church throughout the Middle Ages is intrinsic to the development of the myth of the modern beast. What was once ... a highly revered and worshipped beast, emerges in the medieval period as a savage creature, poisonous, destructive and wholly evil; a beast to be feared and not imitated."[61]

Perhaps one of the most important reasons the Middle Ages began seeing werewolves as malevolent monsters, much

---

[61] Beresford 88. However, in this passage, he does not seem to wholly take into account just how many medieval werewolf legends existed, and how some of them were not necessarily demonic – these were, however, more often than not, unrelated to the Church (except for a few cases, which Beresford himself also cites in his book), so his point largely still stands.

as they are still seen today in popular culture, is due to the stamp of evil put upon wolves and all their kin during this time period, and, by the twelfth century, werewolves were almost equivalent to Satanic witches. The wolf became a creature of allegory, cited in nearly every bestiary as being "the devil, who is always envious of mankind, and continually prowls round the sheepfolds of the Church's believers, to kill their souls and to corrupt them,"[62] a symbol of wilderness contesting the goodness of civilization. The stigma of malevolence put upon the wolf in the medieval period naturally carried over to werewolves as well, as the wolf and werewolf alike become "symbol[s] of all the carnal, bestial wrongs of society, from which God alone can protect Man,"[63] particularly because "[i]n

---

[62] Barber 70, a translation of a 13th-century manuscript. Bestiaries were, in part, intended to relate the symbolism of certain animals, as the Church frequently said that animals are each representations of different sins or virtues. Thus, some animals should be looked to and upheld for their positive aspects and behaviors, which represented some Christian virtue, whereas other animals embodied sin and should be shunned and avoided. Although the wolf, in earlier times, was often seen as a positive creature, much though not all of medieval Christian doctrine disagreed.

[63] Beresford 105

Holy Writ the wolf is ever the emblem of treachery, savagery, and bloodthirstiness."[64]

When the question arose as to whether or not someone with a soul could be transformed into something they are not (specifically, an animal or animal-like creature), the belief in werewolves had such a strong hold over society that not even the Church could entirely stamp it out. In 1487, the *Malleus Maleficarum*, or the *Hammer of Witches*, stated that it was impossible for a man "to be transformed into any shape or likeness, except by the Creator Himself."[65] However, people disputed even this official doctrine by the Church, as powerful as werewolf beliefs were at the time, and the assertion that werewolf transformation is impossible did not hold much power over the people of the Middle Ages. Thomas Malory alludes to werewolves in his *Morte d'Arthur*, two years before the

---

[64] Summers, *Werewolf* 65

[65] Summers, *Malleus* 111. This is quoted from Summers's translation of *The Malleus Maleficarum*. In this chapter, Chapter VIII, the *Malleus Maleficarum* discusses "Of the Manner whereby they Change Men into the Shapes of Beasts," referring to witches. The chapter discusses at length the idea that anyone can take on an animal shape, quoting the Bible and discussing instances of transformation therein, but werewolves are never explicitly mentioned.

Malleus Maleficarum was published, highlighting the normalcy of someone believing in werewolves.[66] Perhaps most notably, the Swiss physician Paracelsus claimed that all humans have a spirit divided into two parts: a human spirit and an animal spirit, and that if a person behaved malevolently in life, his spirit "would be released in the form of a wolf, cat or bear."[67] Christianity led to different portrayals and even scientific and

---

[66] Beresford 108. He quotes a passage from Malory, which says, "Sir Marrok was a good knyghte, that was bitrayed with his wyf, for she made hym seuen yere a werwolf." Interestingly, seven years is a very common amount of time for one to be a werewolf, as seen in other medieval legends, as well, much in the way that the Arcadian werewolf legends have werewolf transformations lasting certain numbers of years at a time.

[67] Beresford 108. This also indicates that bears were increasingly seen as malevolent, like wolves, although bears were also often seen as not harmful or even benevolent in some earlier legends. Whatever the case, bears have certainly never suffered under the same level of harsh stigmas as have wolves (which applies even today, as will be discussed later in this study). Cats and their association with witchcraft and malevolence is an entirely different, and very broad, topic; however, the irony should not be lost that cats today, while needlessly construed as negative quite often, are still seen in a more positive light than wolves, despite the fact that dogs (animals descended from wolves) are, statistically, more popular pets than cats, and cats themselves still suffer from very foolish and baseless stigmas.

theological studies of werewolves in the later Middle Ages, particularly during the sixteenth century, during which werewolves became associated with insanity more than witchcraft and legend – but this will be a topic for the next chapter in this study.

Of course, there are also many other examples of werewolves throughout Europe during the entirety of the Middle Ages, and while some certainly changed under the influence of Christian doctrine, others seemed largely unaffected by it, and a few even defied the traditional Christian view of werewolves as demonic (something that also formed stronger roots in the later medieval periods and into the Early Modern era, more than in the Middle Ages themselves). There exist a few examples of Christians portraying werewolves in a positive light, such as a Mercian priest named Werwulfhum, mentioned in Asser's *De Rebus Gestis Aelfredi*.[68] Another prime example appears in the *Topographia Hibernica* by Giraldus Cambrensis,[69] written in 1187, in a section entitled "Of the

---

[68] Beresford 58

[69] Giraldus Cambrensis, also called Gerald of Wales, was a Welch cleric and chaplain to Henry II. *Topographia Hibernica* is the longest

Prodigies of our Times, and First of a Wolf Which Conversed With a Priest." In this section, Giraldus relates what he calls history rather than legend, in which a wolf approaches a traveling priest and his young companion as they rest by their fire one night. The wolf speaks, telling them not to be afraid, and "add[ing] some orthodox words referring to God."[70] The exchanges of the priest and the wolf are detailed, during which the wolf behaves with Christian grace and manners, telling the priest that he and another woman are '"natives of Ossory, who, through the curse of one Natalis, saint and abbot, are compelled every seven years to put off the human form, and depart from the dwellings of men. Quitting entirely the human form, we assume that of wolves."[71] The wolf has come to beg the priest to aid his sick and dying partner, and he leads the priest to a she-wolf, whom the wolf reveals to be a human as he "tore off the skin of the she-wolf, from the head down to the navel, folding it back. Thus she immediately presented the form of an

---

source on Ireland from the Middle Ages, and it is one of the most influential.

[70] Cambrensis 57

[71] Cambrensis 57

old woman."[72] In gratitude for the priest's help, the wolf watches over him for the night and leads him out of the woods in the morning. Giraldus later says in the same account, "[W]e find that at God's bidding, to exhibit his power and righteous judgment, human nature assumed that of a wolf. But is such an animal to be called a brute or a man? ... We reply, that divine miracles are not to be made the subjects of disputation by human reason, but to be admired."[73] Thus, Giraldus expresses no negative opinions of werewolves, at least as he describes them in his particular account, calling their transformation an act of God rather than an act of the Devil.

In another Christian account, the story of fourteenth-century Saint Francis of Assisi, the Saint travels to Gubbio, in Italy, where he tames a wolf in an allegorical story of Christian doctrine. A wolf killing livestock began to kill humans, until it eventually would eat nothing but human flesh, and the beast was impervious to all attempts to kill it. However, Saint Francis approached the wolf and addressed it, saying, "Come hither,

---

[72] Cambrensis 58

[73] Cambrensis 59

brother wolf; I command thee, in the name of Christ, neither to harm me nor anybody else."[74] The wolf obeyed, lying at his feet, and he told the wolf what evils he had committed, but pardoned him, saying "it is hunger which has made thee do so much evil,"[75] commanding that the wolf will do good so long as he is not driven to evil by hunger. The wolf, "bowing his head, and, by motions of his tail and of his ears,"[76] told Saint Francis he agreed, becoming a beloved friend and companion to all the townsfolk, visiting each home to receive food and kindness. Saint Francis's conversion of the wolf from evil to good highlights that not all Christian accounts showed wolves as hopelessly evil beasts, and the same held true for werewolves, although such sympathetic wolf stories became less common over time.

Other werewolf legends from the Middle Ages – of which there are far too many to consolidate and list in their entirety, at least for the purposes of this study – did not

---

[74] Beresford 103

[75] Beresford 104

[76] Beresford 104

necessarily portray werewolves as malevolent; more often than not, they were helpful, or at least not inherently malicious. Olaus Magnus, Archbishop of Uppsala in Sweden,[77] mentions werewolves in his writing, including one tale wherein a werewolf peasant traveling with a nobleman offered to fetch him a lamb from a nearby flock, "if all the rest would hold their tongues as to what he should do."[78] Famished, the nobleman agreed, and the peasant then transformed into a wolf, brought the noblemen and the other peasants a lamb, and returned to his human form. In *History of the Northern Peoples*, Olaus Magnus mentions that there exists a "species of [wolves] who are transformed from men, and which Pliny confidently says we should account false and fabulous ... [but they] are to be found 'in great abundance' in more notherly countries."[79]

One of the countries specifically mentioned by Olaus Magnus is Livonia, a land along the eastern Baltic Sea, which has quite a few surviving werewolf tales, including some of the most outright "benevolent werewolf" legends during the

---

[77] Beresford 108

[78] Baring-Gould, *Book* 26

[79] Beresford 108

Middle Ages. One Livonian story concerns the wife of a nobleman voicing her doubt to a slave that it is possible "for man or woman thus to change shape."[80] However, her servant said he could prove it is possible, and he left, transforming into a wolf, having his eye torn out while in his lupine form, and then returning to her minus that same eye. Records of Livonian court trials also indicate that there were werewolves and werewolf-like creatures who actually fought to protect innocents and defeat evil beings, including the *Benandanti* ("those who journey to the Blessed Realm") and Livonian werewolves, who were said to battle witches.[81]

Several more stories exist that do not necessarily state that werewolves are malevolent, nor do they portray werewolves as mindless or exceedingly violent creatures. For instance, an interesting Irish tale from the medieval period coincides with the Arcadian rituals from ancient times, in which Saint Patrick supposedly transformed Vereticus, a king

---

[80] Baring-Gould, *Book* 26

[81] Beresford 102. It should be noted that legends of the *benandanti* concern surrounding scholarly controversy as to their true nature, which I shall not bother diving into here.

of Wales, into a wolf. Also, the abbot Saint Natalis put a curse upon "an illustrious family in Ireland; in consequence of which, every male and female take the form of wolves for seven years and live in the forests and career over the bogs, howling mournfully, and appeasing their hunger upon the sheep of the peasants."[82] This curse of Natalis's is the very same mentioned in the account of Giraldus Cambrensis, in which – as previously detailed – these cursed individuals are portrayed as being good and Christian, despite their wolf form.

However, of all werewolf tales to come out of the medieval period, perhaps some of the most influential of all are stories that – arguably – no one ever believed as true: court tales and Breton lais, including *Bisclavret*, *Melion*, *Bisclarel*, *Arthur and Gorlagon*, and *Guillaume de Palerne*, all of which used the word "werewolf" for a sympathetic and noble being, even though they were written around the same time as the ecclesiastical writings that condemned werewolves as demons.[83] Many of these texts are extremely similar in terms of

---

[82] Baring-Gould, *Book* 27

[83] These writings date from various time periods: *Bisclavret* during the early or mid twelfth century, *Melion* from around 1190-1204, *Bisclarel*

the story and the morals conveyed therein: the werewolf in each tale is an innocent individual who was wronged by a woman and either becomes a werewolf or is stuck in werewolf form because of the evil acts of a lady. Perhaps the most popular and well-known of these tales is Marie de France's *Bisclavret*, or simply "The Werewolf," in which a noble werewolf knight falls in love with a woman, but upon telling her he is a werewolf, she traps him in his wolf form. Bisclavret, as a wolf, finds the king and treats him with such grace and nobility that the king takes him in; when Bisclavret attacks his wife, she tells the king the truth and he demands she allow Bisclavret to return to his human form. *Melion* tells almost the very same tale as *Bisclavret*, in which a knight in King Arthur's court turns into a wolf using a magic ring, in order to retrieve stag meat for a woman who claims she will die without it; however, the woman runs away with the ring and traps Melion in his wolf form, who is only rescued when King Arthur hears of the deed and demands the

---

from around 1319-1342, *Arthur and Gorlagon* from the fourteenth century, and *Guillaume de Palerne* from around 1220. This means that *Bisclavret* would have been written around the very same time as King Cnut provided us with the first recorded use of the word "werewolf."

ring back in order to cure Melion. *Bisclarel* is almost certainly a reworking of *Bisclavret*, particularly given its title, as the tale is almost exactly the same, with one of the few differences being that the king is instead specifically King Arthur. *Arthur and Gorlagon* tells the very same tale again, but this time within a frame story of King Arthur seeking to understand women. He meets Gorlagon, who tells him a story almost exactly like *Bisclavret* and the other sympathetic werewolf tales, and in the end of the frame story, Gorlagon tells Arthur that he himself was the werewolf. Lastly, *Guillaume de Palerne* stands apart from the others in that the werewolf in the story has been transformed through a curse put upon him by his stepmother, and he aids two young, royal lovers who have become fugitives. Once the heroes defeat the villain and win back their kingdom, the curse upon the werewolf is removed.

Of all these tales, *Bisclavret* may be the most interesting to examine and undoubtedly the most influential.[84] Perhaps

---

[84] *Bisclavret* came before the other tales, and thus almost certainly influenced them, especially considering the subject matter. Today, it is uncommon to hear about almost any of these stories, but if one hears any of these titles, it will almost certainly be *Bisclavret*, especially as it was written by Marie de France, whose lays provide historians

the most outstanding difference *Bisclavret* shows from the other werewolf tales is that the werewolf is not truly "cured" of his lycanthropy, at least not in the same way. Instead of being cursed into a permanent wolf form or using a magic spell or item to transform into a wolf, Bisclavret is a werewolf initially, and we have no reason to believe he will not continue his regular werewolf transformations even after the story is finished. Marie de France opens her tale by discussing werewolves, saying, "Such beasts as he [the werewolf] are known in every land. Bisclavaret he is named in Brittany, whilst the Norman calls him Garwal."[85] Marie de France seems to find werewolves common enough, at least in terms of this story, as she remarks, "It is a certain thing, and within the knowledge of all, that many a christened man has suffered this change, and ran wild in the woods, as a Were-Wolf."[86] Although she describes a werewolf as "a fearsome beast,"[87] the werewolf in her tale reflects none of the evil and violent qualities she

---

with a look into medieval life and culture, even if they are fantastical.

[85] de France 256

[86] de France 256

[87] de France 256

describes initially. In *Bisclavret*, the werewolf requires his clothing to return to a human form, as he sheds this same clothing before each transformation, and the transformations occur "three whole days in every week."[88] In the end of the story, when the knight's clothes are returned to him and he can return to his human form, the king – who has, all this time, taken care of the noble werewolf – finds him in human form: "The King ran swiftly to the bed and taking his friend in his arms, embraced and kissed him fondly, above a hundred times."[89] The King later showers the knight in gifts and returns his land to him, casting out his treacherous wife and displaying absolutely no concern regarding the knight's future werewolf transformations, which will clearly continue as they always had. Although Marie de France opens her tale with descriptions of werewolves that "goeth to and fro, about the solitary place, seeking man, in order to devour him,"[90] the werewolf in her story is a truly chivalrous, loyal, and noble baron who displays every virtue desirable in a courtly knight, making *Bisclavret* the

---

[88] de France 256

[89] de France 261

[90] de France 256

quintessential werewolf tale of the noble, sympathetic, and even benevolent werewolf that appears in medieval tales.

Werewolves in the Middle Ages abound in so many legends across so many regions that it is impossible to encompass them all without writing a very large book dedicated to that sole purpose. However, these examples provide an overview of the werewolf of the medieval world: both those stories of the Middle Ages that portray the werewolf as a sympathetic, even noble, individual instead of a ravening monster, as well as those stories and beliefs that convey the growing shift to seeing werewolves as malevolent. It is with good reason that the Middle Ages is the era many often consider to be the time of the werewolf, even as untrue as it may be, given that it was the late Middle Ages and the Renaissance during which werewolves entered the minds of scholars and scientists and came under the strongest scrutiny by the Church and those seeking explanations for a belief in werewolves, and werewolf legends were told long before the medieval era. However, as the early Middle Ages gave way to a world, especially a European world, dominated by a modernized and less localized Church controlling laws, working in tandem with scientific rationale about folklore, stronger governments that detested all things wild and untamed, and an increase in scientific thought and search for rational truths, the view of the werewolf changed yet again. Instead of being an individual who undergoes a physical transformation into a wolf – whether this is accomplished through means of a magic skin, ring, ointment, or other object; a curse; an inherited condition; a regularly-induced transformation, the origin of which is not specified; or a transformation set upon one by God or even the Devil – the werewolf instead is viewed, more often than not, in one of two ways: a product of witchcraft or insanity. In some cases, the werewolf may be described as an evil witch using Satanic magic to transform, who can neither have nor retain any chivalrous behavior – and, indeed, it should be noted that it is because of werewolf scholars that these witches came to be perceived as werewolves at all by modern scholarship, even if they were not referred to as such during their own time periods. More commonly, however, as will be seen in the records of numerous werewolf court trials that abounded in later periods, particularly sixteenth-century France, the werewolf is said to be nothing more than a madman.

Chapter III – Werewolves Go Mad: The Transition into Modernity

As seen in the previous chapter, during the early and middle Middle Ages, Church doctrine, mostly in the form of law, began to dictate that werewolves were malevolent creatures aligned with the Devil himself, but stories and accounts – many of them Christian in nature – still abounded portraying the wolf and werewolf as sympathetic, and in some cases, still noble and kind. However, by the later Middle Ages and into the Renaissance period, science and law worked in tandem with the Church to reinforce the idea that werewolves could never be morally acceptable. All across Europe – and perhaps particularly in France – as governments and the Church, at this time very closely tied together, became more powerful, people were put on trial under accusations of witchcraft and werewolfery, and the idea of the werewolf came under great scrutiny and criticism. Scholars and scientists also turned their interest to the supernatural, studying the would-be werewolves and attempting to justify mankind's widespread belief in their existence while also passing judgment on the werewolves of their time period, working alongside the Church and vice versa. During this era began the connections between werewolves and madmen, as – despite the outstanding opinions and views of many individuals, even some theologians – the Church and scientists alike, not at odds as they are often thought to be today, ultimately found that the only reasonable explanation for the legend of the werewolf was insanity.

For the entirety of the Middle Ages and into the Early Modern period, France represented a region in which werewolf legends thrived more than almost any other, compared even to Germany. In fact, although some sources indicate that the idea of a werewolf transforming at the full moon began in Greece, southern regions of France – even into the 1800s[91] – believed

---

[91] Baring-Gould mentions this in his *Book of Were-Wolves*, written during the 1800s. His intention with the book was to find people who still believed in werewolves (the belief was still widespread during this time, and meeting those who warned him of a werewolf nearby inspired him to research werewolves in the first place) and argue that werewolves do not, and cannot, exist. He found people throughout Europe (including in France, Greece, and Eastern Europe) who still believed in the werewolf during his time.

that werewolves "transformed into wolves at the full moon. The desire to run comes upon them at night."[92] It is only fitting, then, that in the later Middle Ages during the sixteenth century, France practically became the seat of werewolf trials. As time passed, researchers began to declare that being a werewolf was a form of madness. Specifically, the term "lycanthropy" came to be used as referring to a mental disease, particularly by those eager to disprove the idea that werewolves could ever be real, such as Sabine Baring-Gould: "It was not till the close of the Middle Ages that lycanthropy was recognized as a disease."[93] It was in France, then, that one of the most famous of the werewolf court trials took place.

In 1603, in France, a supposed werewolf by the name of Jean Grenier ravaged the countryside, and Sabine Baring-Gould retold Jean Grenier's case in a rather extrapolated version of the story, written as a non-fictional narrative, instead of republishing it in its original form as a case study and a trial record. Baring-Gould most likely fictionalized

---

[92] Baring-Gould, *Book* 46

[93] Baring-Gould, *Book* 56

certain events – namely the detailed dialogue between Grenier and some of his victims – since what is known about Grenier is simple: he was a madman, who at the age of fourteen admitted that he "had sold himself to the devil, and that he had acquired the power of ranging the country after dusk, and sometimes in broad day, in the form of a wolf."[94] Grenier also admitted to devouring several children, since "the flesh of little girls ... he regarded as supreme delicacy."[95] In court, he told his story: "When I was ten or eleven years old, my neighbour ... introduced me, in the depths of the forest, to a M. de la Forest, a black man, who signed me with his nail, and then gave to me ... a salve and a wolf skin. From that time I have run about the country as a wolf."[96] Grenier's description of the devil-worshiper who signed his pact with the Devil as "black" must be discussed, as he most likely did not intend the description to refer to someone of African descent, given that medical accounts of this period often described European lycanthropy

---

[94] Baring-Gould, "Jean" 64

[95] Baring-Gould, "Jean" 64

[96] Baring-Gould, "Jean" 65

victims as being black or dark in complexion due to assorted diseases: thus, this would provide another connection between this individual and other werewolf beliefs of the time period. However, not enough is known about this M. de la Forest figure to assume his heritage. Grenier's werewolf transformations are very different from anything featured in other legends, as he actually transformed "when the moon was at the wane,"[97] instead of when it was full, and he said that the "Lord of the Forest had strictly forbidden him to bite the thumb-nail of his left hand, and had warned him never to lose sight of it, as long as he was in his were-wolf disguise."[98] In this case, the court decided "that Lycanthropy ... [is] mere hallucination ... and that the change of shape existed only in the disorganized brain of the insane, consequently it was not a crime which could be punished."[99] Ultimately, Grenier was sentenced "to perpetual imprisonment within the walls of a monastery at Bordeaux,

---

[97] Baring-Gould, "Jean" 66

[98] Baring-Gould, "Jean" 66

[99] Baring-Gould, "Jean" 67. These statements highlight the fact that lycanthropy, at this point in history, is increasingly viewed only as madness.

where he might be instructed in his Christian and moral obligations, but any attempt to escape would be punished with death."[100] Grenier, however, never recovered from his insanity, and he "ran frantically about ... upon all fours,"[101] devouring raw meat and behaving strangely. At the age of twenty, after seven years in confinement, he died, and he was described around the time of his death as "diminutive ... very shy, and unwilling to look anyone in the face. His eyes were deep set and restless, his teeth long and protruding, his nails black, and in places worn away, his mind was completely barren, he seemed unable to comprehend the smallest things."[102]

Much like France, Germany is a region from which popular culture has received many of its ideas about werewolves, and also like France, Germany was home to one of the most historic of supposed werewolf trials (though it was never referred to as a "werewolf" trial during its own time period, and this moniker was later wrongfully put upon it by

---

[100] Baring-Gould, "Jean" 67

[101] Baring-Gould, "Jean" 67

[102] Baring-Gould, "Jean" 68

werewolf scholars): Peter Stubbe, who was tried in 1589.[103] The original transcript of the trial begins by saying that Stubbe "from his youth was greatly inclined to evil and the practising of wicked arts, surfeiting in the damnable desires of magic, necromancy, and sorcery, acquainting himself with many infernal spirits and fiends."[104] According to the transcript, the Devil gave Stubbe a girdle that allowed him to turn into "the likeness of a greedy, devouring wolf, strong and mighty, with eyes great and large, which in the night sparkled like brands of fire, a mouth great and wide, with most sharp and cruel teeth, a huge body and mighty paws."[105] When he removed the belt, he returned to his human form. Stubbe committed numerous atrocities using his wolf shape, and he even raped several women in his human form before killing them as a wolf,[106] marking the first instance anything scholars today equate to a werewolf has been associated with rape (despite what some

---

[103] Also called Stubbe Peeter, Peter Stumpp, Peter Stube, or Peeter Stubbe, as well as various spellings of Abal Griswold.

[104] "Stubbe" 69

[105] "Stubbe" 69

[106] "Stubbe" 70

movies of today may indicate).[107] Likewise, Stubbe popularized the association between werewolves and cannibalism, as the account mentions he "ate their [his victims'] hearts panting hot and raw, which he accounted dainty morsels and best agreeing to his appetite."[108]

Indeed, the account of Peter Stubbe lists so many unspeakable atrocities that he alone may have caused the great shift from the conception of werewolves as sympathetic to that of werewolves as wholly malevolent. Stubbe's crimes not only included rape and cannibalism, but murdering animals to eat

---

[107] Werewolves have **never** been a symbol of rape. Although some horror movies and stories of today (and especially of the 1980s, as shall be discussed later in this study) use werewolves as symbols of sexual deviants and rapists, this development has never been indicated in ancient legend, and Stubbe's trial record created the single arguable connection between rape and lycanthropy in any historical and/or mythological account (though, as further detailed, Stubbe was technically referred to as a "sorcerer," and not a "werewolf"). At their very worst and most malevolent in legends, werewolves were symbols of gluttony, ferocity, violence, cunning, bloodlust, and sometimes cannibalism (although this was only in a very few later stories; earlier stories used werewolves as a means to highlight the humanity of the cursed individual in that they resisted eating another human's flesh), but never sexual offenses.

[108] "Stubbe" 70

raw "as if he had been a natural wolf indeed;"[109] killing pregnant women and tearing their children from the womb; committing acts of incest with his family and even his own daughter, with whom he had a child; and killing his own son and eating his brains. The account mentions that "oftentimes the inhabitants [of Germany] found the arms and legs of dead men, women, and children scattered up and down the fields, ... knowing the same had to be done by that strange and cruel wolf, whom by no means they could overcome."[110] After rampaging for twenty-five years, he was captured only because he removed his girdle and transformed back into a man at an inopportune time: he was seen transforming, and as he could not be defeated as a wolf, he was apprehended as a man. After being tortured on a rack, before he could be tortured further, he confessed to all his crimes, most importantly to the girdle given to him by the Devil. For his crimes, Stubbe received a brutal execution by "first to have his body laid on a wheel, and with red hot burning pincers in ten places to have the flesh pulled off from the bones,

---

[109] "Stubbe" 70

[110] "Stubbe" 73

after that, his legs and arms to be broken with a wooden axe or hatchet, afterward to have his head struck from his body, then to have his carcase burned to ashes."[111] A monument, including a carving of a wolf in the wheel upon which he was executed and also featuring Stubbe's own head on a stake, was erected in order to warn others of the fate he suffered for his sins.

However, the account of Peter Stubbe and his association with werewolves is questionable today for many reasons, not least of which is that Stubbe is referred to only as a "sorcerer," and *never* as a "werewolf." The very title of the account describes Stubbe as "A Most Wicked Sorcerer, Who in the Likeness of a Wolf Committed Many Murders."[112] Likewise, Stubbe's actions do not bear many similarities to those told in previous werewolf tales, highlighting the fact that he is more a sorcerer than a werewolf: he was tried and convicted of "sorcery,"[113] with no mention made of lycanthropy in his entire trial – and no mention of insanity of any form. Other trials of

---

[111] "Stubbe" 75

[112] "Stubbe" 69

[113] "Stubbe" 74

the time did indeed specify lycanthropy or werewolfism, but not his. Stubbe was convicted as a truly malevolent man, who committed his crimes solely out of a desire to do evil and derive pleasure from it, going so far as to make a pact with the devil. Even madmen convicted of lycanthropy – whether as a clinical disease and a form of insanity or as "true" shapeshifting – were offered more sympathy than was extended to Stubbe. Therefore, although the influence Stubbe's trial account exerts over certain werewolves in popular culture today is all too unfortunately apparent,[114] it is certainly inaccurate and even seems almost unfair to use this trial as any kind of basis for werewolves. Unlike other werewolves who were not referred to as "werewolves," such as King Lycaon,[115] the detail that Stubbe turns into a wolf holds no particular significance: he could have just as easily turned into a lion or some other predatory animal. King Lycaon's wolf transformation was intended as a punishment and an irony, given his name and the beliefs of his

---

[114] Such as the sexually obsessed werewolves of *The Howling* film.

[115] As seen in Chapter I of this study. It is noteworthy, of course, that the term "werewolf" and its equivalents had not yet come into existence, in ancient Greek or not.

people, but Stubbe's wolf form does little other than provide wolves with a bad name. While many werewolf stories are referred to only as "werewolf" legends and accounts much later, since Stubbe's account was written during a time period in which the terms "werewolf" and "lycanthropy" were both used and yet neither term is seen in reference to him or his trial, Stubbe should be viewed as a sorcerer rather than a werewolf. Stubbe's account has no place among werewolf accounts or lycanthropy trials, as his connection with wolves serves less as an example of a belief in werewolves, and more as an example of a belief in witchcraft, as well as offering another example in which wolves are cast in a malevolent light, thanks to an association of them with the Devil. Consequently, today's scholars are inaccurate in terming as "werewolves" those sorcerers who only turned into wolves but otherwise were never said to be "werewolves." If people of the era believed people like Peter Stubbe to be "werewolves," instead of sorcerers, they would have identified them as such, since terms for werewolves existed at this point in history, unlike in the stories from ages past that we now call "werewolf legends."

Through witchcraft, sorcerers turned into a great many animals, including wolves and cats, yet we do not find scholars referring to witches turning into cats as "werecats."[116]

In line with the assorted other late medieval accounts of werewolves as madmen, some events in 1541 further reflect the changing ideas of who and what exactly was a "werewolf," as werewolves of the later Middle Ages were not always believed to undergo a physical transformation. In events recounted by Montague Summers,[117] a peasant in Pavia, Italy, went mad believing himself to be a wolf, and he attacked a group of fellow peasants in a field, lashing out at them with his teeth, rending their flesh, and killing several. He was – with

[116] Of course, it is important to note that the term "werecat" in itself is a modern contrivance. In ancient folklore, the term "werewolf" is unique among shapeshifters, and any contemporary derivatives for other shapeshifter legends ("werebears," "werecats," etc.) owe their very modern and contrived etymology to the ancient term "werewolf." These terms do not really have a place in folklore studies and generally serve to, in popular culture, refer to some takeoff of werewolves that simply turns into something other than a wolf, instead of taking into account any legends of people turning into cats or any other animal in question.

[117] He credits the account of these events to one Job Fincel, a humanist and physician alive during the mid-1500s.

great difficulty, according to accounts – finally captured, but he refused to give up his delusion of being a wolf. The peasant told his captors that "whereas wolves are hairy outside, my fur grows within my body."[118] Bystanders made deep wounds in his arms and legs to investigate the truth behind this, and the peasant was later taken to physicians, but he died in their care. This account provides one of the most overt references to werewolves having fur that grows under their skin, which is a relatively obscure belief in werewolf lore that nonetheless appeared in some plays in the late medieval and Early Modern eras. It is, however, noteworthy to mention that the man who wrote the account of the mad peasant clearly felt sympathy for him in his insanity. After the peasant mentioned the fur under his skin, Fincel described the bystanders who attacked him as "showing themselves to be more cruel wolves than he" when they mortally wounded him in order to find the truth,[119] which is, of course, yet another reference to how wolves were – and, in many cases, still are – seen to be evil creatures.

---

[118] Summers, *Werewolf* 160-161

[119] Summers, *Werewolf* 161

Of the many werewolf court cases heard in the 1600s, however, perhaps the most unusual is one in which the accused werewolf proclaimed that he and his kin were benevolent in nature. Willem de Blécourt discusses this particular court case in his article "A Journey to Hell: Reconsidering the Livonian 'Werewolf,'" in which he stresses a need for scholars to investigate beyond the modern portrayal of insane werewolves. The court case in question occurred in 1691 in present-day Latvia, and the would-be werewolf in question was named Thies of Kaltenbrun. Initially, the case concerned a church robbery, but then the court was informed that Thies "consorted with the devil and was a werewolf."[120] Surprising the court, Thies admitted to being a werewolf in the past, and he said he broke his nose in Hell when he traveled there with other werewolves, in order to retrieve some grain. Thies had told this to the court once before and they laughed him off, but this second testimony of lycanthropy concerned them, particularly as "several people present in court ... knew him well [and] said that his common sense had never failed him. It also emerged

---

[120] Blécourt 49

that his status had risen since his previous encounter with the law."[121] Of all the details around Thies's case, the most important distinction between his story and that of other werewolves is that Thies declared werewolves to be benevolent. When told werewolves were allies of the Devil, Thies disputed this, saying that werewolves battled Satanic wizards in hell, and werewolves were the Hounds of God: "The souls of the werewolves went to heaven while those of the wizards were seized by the devil. Thus the werewolves only went to hell to recapture cattle, grain, fruit, and fish in order to ensure a good crop for the coming year."[122] Thies was also a local healer, who blessed crops and animals, as well as casting charms against wolves. It was for his blessings that the court decided he was sacrilegious, as his blessings did not mention God (although Thies himself said he was a Christian, and in these blessings "God simply was not mentioned"[123]). Therefore, the judges

---

[121] Blécourt 49

[122] Blécourt 50. Note the difference between, and the specificity of, werewolves and witches/sorcerers, which were not perceived to be the same thing.

[123] Blécourt 50

"sentenced [Thies] to be flogged and banished for life."[124] As Blécourt himself states in this same article, "The primary scholarship on werewolves was developed on the basis of French demonological treatises."[125] Such medical examinations dismissed all ancient belief about werewolves as shamans and healers, or any kind of benevolent figure at all, as did the Church when judging werewolves on the basis of Satanic witchcraft, but physicians cast werewolves as pathetically insane individuals, much as did the court that judged Jean Grenier. As Adam Douglas said in *The Beast Within*, "the essential role of diagnosing who was a 'witch' or a 'werewolf' began to pass from the judge to the physician. The process is clearly marked at the end of the era of werewolf trials in sixteenth century France."[126]

During the late 1500s and early 1600s, as werewolves that underwent true, physical transformations were no longer being accepted as real by institutions such as the Church, physicians began to hold more sway over how a suspected

---

[124] Blécourt 50

[125] Blécourt 50

[126] Douglas 260

werewolf was judged. Many authors, including Reginald Scot, Henri Boguet, King James I of England, John Deacon and John Walker, I. Goulart, Robert Burton, and Robert Bayfield, described lycanthropy as a medical condition, generally boiled down to melancholy. Though the accounts from these various physicians, demonologists, and other influential individuals vary slightly, they seem to have taken elements from one another over time, in order to shape the general conception of what is, today, termed "clinical lycanthropy."

The first of these many investigations into the true nature of werewolves, entitled "Of Transformations," was written in 1584, by agriculturalist[127] Reginald Scot in *The Discoverie of Witchcraft*. Although more of a theological or spiritual approach to explaining the werewolf than a medical one, Scot's work nonetheless has been used by many scholars as a look into werewolf beliefs of the late 1500s. Scot opens his first chapter with the very blatant summary, "Of transformations, ridiculous examples brought by the

---

[127] Otten xi

adversaries for the confirmation of their foolish doctrine."[128]
Scot investigates several examples brought to him of
"*Lycanthropia*"[129] throughout the chapters of his book,
ultimately deciding that "the transformations, which these
witch-mongers doo so rave and rage upon, is (as all the learned
sort of physicians affirme) a disease proceeding partlie from
melancholie, wherebie manie suppose themselves to be
woolves."[130] Therefore, Scot paved the way for other physicians
reiterating the idea of this time period that all werewolves, past
and present, originated from a melancholic disease or
disorder.

In 1590, Henri Boguet, demonologist and Chief Justice
of Saint-Claude,[131] wrote "Of the Metamorphosis of Men into
Beasts" in his *Discours des Sorciers*, in which he recounts many
different trial records of werewolves and examines his own
beliefs regarding "Of the Metamorphosis of Men into Beasts,

---

[128] Scot 115

[129] Scot 115

[130] Scot 126

[131] Otten ix

and Especially of Lycanthropes or Loups-garoux."[132] As a preface for his examination regarding whether or not he believes wolf transformation to be real, Boguet lists many historical instances of people turning into wolves, such as the legends of Arcadia, the account of Job Fincel, accounts of Herodotus, and more, such as how "[w]hen the Romans were trying to prevent Hannibal from crossing the Alps, a wolf came amongst their army, rent those whom it met, and finally escaped without being hurt," ultimately ending his discussion by asking, "Who, then, can doubt but that these wolves were Lycanthropes?"[133]   However, Boguet marks a difference between werewolves and witches that have turned into wolves, repeating a common belief that, when witches turn into animals, they have "no tails,"[134] unlike werewolves. Later,

---

[132] Boguet 77

[133] Boguet 79

[134] Boguet 79. This, of course, implies that werewolves *do* have tails, according to folkloric beliefs, and it is outright stated in many works throughout folklore and myth that werewolves do have tails. It is one of their hallmark frightening and inhuman features. Many modern depictions of werewolves have long since forgotten this once-important distinction, and werewolves of popular culture that lack tails are becoming increasingly common, which speaks to the lack of

Boguet again changes his mind and decides werewolves and witches are the same thing, directly contradicting himself. Over the course of his discussion, Boguet tends to indicate his disbelief, questioning the idea of lycanthropy being real: "Nevertheless it has always been my opinion that Lycanthropy is an illusion, and that the metamorphosis of a man into a beast is impossible."[135] To Boguet, it becomes a matter of what happens to the werewolf's soul when it transforms, as he does not believe a soul can either return to a body if the beast form goes mad, or that a human soul can inhabit the body of a beast if the werewolf retains his sanity. However, Boguet does not question this idea as a scientist, but a theologian, who refuses to believe that the soul could undergo such changes, even while admitting that the *body* physically could. Regardless of Boguet's

---

research performed by most writers and designers of werewolves – or at least the lack of respect and interest most folklore receives today, despite its importance in history. It may also, of course, speak to the lack of budget given to werewolf films, especially with the stigma surrounding them in Hollywood. However, arguments can still be made regarding why werewolves do not have tails in a lot of media, considering modern audiences do not see having a tail as being a terrifying and inhuman aspect and instead is often seen as being "cute."

[135] Boguet 83

beliefs about the spiritual and physical, he too considers only one possibility: that werewolves are malevolent creatures of madness, concluding his work with the judgment, "I should be sorry to leave this subject without reprimanding those who would excuse them [werewolves] and cast the blame for all that they do upon Satan, as if they were entirely innocent."[136]

Although not medical in nature, perhaps one of the most interesting treatises on werewolves from the late Middle Ages is "Men-Woolfes," not necessarily because of any important statements therein, but simply because the treatise was written in 1597 by King James I of England. Originally from his book *Daemonologie*, King James I wrote a section addressing lycanthropy to respond to it as an issue. When asked about his opinion on "war-woolfes," King James I replied that he found it to be "but of a naturall super-abundance of Melancholie."[137] Although only a brief section, the fact that lycanthropy was of such importance that King James I felt the need to address it certainly signifies that it was a legitimate concern for many

---

[136] Boguet 90

[137] James I 128

centuries.

The English preachers[138] John Deacon and John Walker provided very little explanation for werewolves in their "Spirits and Devils" excerpt from their 1601 *Dialogicall Discourses of Spirits and Divils*, instead dismissing lycanthropy entirely as "illusions and sleights of the devil to deceive."[139] The account is presented in the form of personified Orthodoxy (named Orthodoxus) discussing lycanthropy with two other figures: Philosophy (Philologus) and lycanthropy itself (Lycanthropus). After much discussion, Orthodoxus ultimately declares, "many good writers, yea, and the Popes owne canons do all jointly condemne and pronounce this peevish opinion concerning the supposed transformation of divels, to be impious, absurd and divellish, and the maintainers thereof to be woorse than Infidels."[140] Although werewolves in general are one of many ancient pagan beliefs turned into Satanism by Christianity,[141]

---

[138] Otten x

[139] Deacon 133

[140] Deacon 133

[141] Essentially, every pagan ritual, belief, and myth was either incorporated into acts of God or turned into devil-worship by the rise of Christianity, such as those that were incorporated into holidays to

Deacon and Walker say that someone believing in werewolves is "woorse then a Pagane."[142] The prompting of Orthodoxus and Philologus has Lycanthropus admit, "praising the Lord with all my hart, for bringing me thus to behold the folly thereof: yea, and am hartely sory, for being bewitched therewith so long, being also ashamed now of my odious name."[143] Deacon and Walker do not attribute belief in lycanthropy to madmen, melancholy, or any combination thereof, instead boiling it all down to a devilish illusion of a nonspecific, but certainly sacrilegious, nature.

Perhaps one of the most influential treatises regarding an explanation behind the supposed existence of werewolves is

---

help calm and stabilize local populations, such as Christmas trees and the fertility rituals of the Easter bunny and eggs. Satyrs and other Greek forest spirits became devils, lending the Devil his goat-like depictions with goat legs and horns. However, it was scientific rationalization of folklore that primarily led to werewolves eventually becoming seen as madmen instead of great warriors and noble knights, or sympathetic individuals, or helpful shamans and healers, and familiar spirits became the companions of witches instead of spirits meant to protect and guide individuals. At the very least, one should acknowledge that religion is not *solely* to blame.

[142] Deacon 133

[143] Deacon 133

a section from *Admirable and Memorable Histories* by I. Goulart,[144] published in 1607. Goulart calls werewolves "melancholike," and he says that they "imagine themselves to be transformed into Wolves," accusing them of going out "in Februarie, conterfet Wolves in a manner of all things."[145] Such descriptions of werewolves also hold true in later medical examinations by Robert Burton and Robert Bayfield. However, Goulart distinguishes between different types of lycanthropes: the sick and the Satanists. The former he describes as being very ill, saying that they "are afflicted with that disease, are pale, their eyes are hollow, and they see ill, their tongue is drye, they are much altered, and are without much spittle in the mouth."[146] The latter, however, are "by some particular power of Sathan, they seeme Wolves and not Men."[147] Goulart argues that all occurrences of werewolf legends in history can be divided into these two camps, saying that most werewolves are

---

[144] "French historian, collector of memoirs and journals" (Otten x). His frequent subjects included both medicine and demonology.

[145] Goulart 41

[146] Goulart 42

[147] Goulart 42

"all (as it seemes to them) changed and transformed into Wolves."[148] Goulart himself, however, does not offer his own explanation or opinion as to whether any of these werewolves are truly "real," saying, "But we will leave their controversie to such as will looke into it."[149]

Goulart's medical description of lycanthropy, however, made an impression on least two later authors: Robert Burton, who mentions werewolves in "Diseases of the Mind," included in his 1621 *Anatomy of Melancholy*; and Robert Bayfield, in "A Treatise," written in 1663 in *A treatise De Morborum Capitis Essentiis & Prognosticis.* Burton was a clergyman, whose book *Anatomy of Melancholy* "is an encyclopedic treatment of mental illness, including religious melancholy and love melancholy."[150] However, when Robert Burton mentions lycanthropy in his text *Anatomy of Melancholy*, written in 1621, he questions whether lycanthropy is specifically melancholy, though he does not deny that it is a disease, which he instead calls "Wolf-

---

[148] Goulart 43

[149] Goulart 44

[150] Otten ix

madness."[151] As do other medical texts of the 1600's, Burton specifically designates running and "howling about graves and fields in the night"[152] as qualities of the madmen who suffer from lycanthropy and believe that they are wolves. Burton cites other scholars and authors who discuss the issue, though he does not see lycanthropy as being a "Melancholy," and instead refers to it as a "Madness, as most do."[153] Whether he believes it to be melancholy or some other form of madness, Burton's descriptions correspond with his contemporaries' evaluations stating that werewolves are madmen who stalk graveyards. Bayfield, a British physician who published many books about anatomy, pharmacology, disease, and theology,[154] essentially echoes everything said by Burton, saying, "Wolf-madness, is a disease, in which men run barking and howling about graves and fields in the night ... and will not be persuaded but that they are Wolves."[155] Like previous discussions on the subject,

---

[151] Burton 46

[152] Burton 46

[153] Burton 46

[154] Otten ix

[155] Bayfield 47

Bayfield describes those suffering from "wolf-madness" as having "usually hollow eyes, scabbed legs and thighs, very dry and pale."[156]

Even while under such great scrutiny by scientists and by the Church, or perhaps especially because of it, werewolves continued to appear now and then in fiction of the time period, including various dramas. In *The Duchess of Malfi* by English dramatist John Webster, written in 1612-1613, the villain of the play, Ferdinand, is said to be a werewolf, almost exactly like the werewolves from many trial records, accounts of sightings,[157] and medical records of Webster's time period. Many of the descriptions of Ferdinand and his actions in *Duchess* reflect almost word-for-word descriptions of lycanthropy patients in certain medical accounts, such as those of I. Goulart. For example, Ferdinand's doctor describes lycanthropy – or, as he calls it, lycanthropia – as a disease "In those that are possessed with't there o'erflows / Such melancholy humor they imagine /

---

[156] Bayfield 47

[157] Job Fincel's werewolf account seems to have very heavily influenced Ferdinand's character and some of the lines in *The Duchess of Malfi*.

Themselves to be transformèd into wolves,"[158] and that werewolves "Steal forth to churchyards in the dead of night / And dig dead bodies up."[159] Throughout the play, Ferdinand equates himself and his family members to wolves and seems obsessed with wolfish imagery. At one point, Ferdinand all but proves his lycanthropy when he meets someone on the lane behind a church while carrying "the leg of a man / Upon his shoulder; and he howled fearfully; / Said he was a wolf, only the difference / Was, a wolf's skin was hairy on the outside, / His on the inside."[160]

Likewise, other Elizabethan and Jacobean dramatists have at least made reference to lycanthropy in their plays, though their works are perhaps not as famous as *The Duchess of Malfi*.[161] John Ford mentions werewolves in his 1629 play *The Lover's Melancholy*. A character, Rhetias, enters to recite several lines regarding his insanity, blaming it on lycanthropy and

---

[158] Webster 5.2.8-10

[159] Webster 5.2.11-12

[160] Webster 5.2.14-18

[161] Charlotte F. Otten, editor of *A Lycanthropy Reader*, mentions in the introduction to the book that her first encounter with werewolves was in *The Duchess of Malfi*.

referring to his transformation into a wolf. Stage directions indicate that Rhetias is to enter with *"his face whited, blacke shag haire, long nailes, a piece of raw meate."*[162] Although Ford also refers to elements of werewolf lore not mentioned by Webster, such as "the Moone's eclipsed," he refers to numerous elements found in *Duchess*.[163] For instance, Rhetias, the lycanthropic madman, says he will "to the Church-yard and sup : Since I turn'd Wolfe, I bark and howle, and digge vp graues, ... tis midnight, deepe darke midnight."[164] Rhetias is also found in a churchyard, as is Ferdinand, which is supposedly a common haunt of lycanthropic madmen. A physician in the play, Corax, says of Rhetias's condition, "This kind is called, *Lycanthropia*, Sir, When men conceiue themselues Wolues."[165] In his *The Chronicle Historie of Perkin Warbeck*, written in 1634, John Ford has King Henry's chaplain, Urswicke, make reference to witches turning into wolves – which, although arguably not directly related to lycanthropy or werewolves given that they

---

[162] Summers, Werewolf 161, quoted from The Lover's Melancholy

[163] Summers, Werewolf 161, quoted from The Lover's Melancholy

[164] Summers, Werewolf 161, quoted from The Lover's Melancholy

[165] Summers, Werewolf 162, quoted from The Lover's Melancholy

are not mentioned by name, is nonetheless a reference to the idea of shapeshifting sorcerers, like Peter Stubbe.[166]

The search for the reason behind werewolf legends is not exclusive to the late Middle Ages or Early Modern period, just as widespread belief in werewolves is not exclusive to ancient times and the Middle Ages. The entirety of Sabine Baring-Gould's *The Book of Were-Wolves*, published in 1865, was written as his own personal attempt to prove that a werewolf is nothing more than a delusional madman. Baring-Gould opens his book by describing an encounter with some people just outside of Paris, France, all of whom tell him not to go walking at night for fear of "'the loups-garoux.'"[167] Baring-Gould says, "This was my first introduction to were-wolves, and the circumstance of finding the superstition still so prevalent, first gave me the idea of investigating the history and the habits of these still mythical creatures."[168] Apparently, Baring-Gould set

---

[166] See Summers, *Werewolf* 162. Any variations of terms for werewolves, including "lycanthropy," are not included, leading one to believe that the would-be werewolf here is more just a sorcerer like Stubbe, rather than someone specifically accused of lycanthropy.

[167] Baring-Gould, *Book* 6

[168] Baring-Gould, *Book* 7

out to acquire a werewolf, an attempt which he admits was – unsurprisingly – unsuccessful.[169] Despite sentiments he expresses later in the book, Baring-Gould begins with some skepticism about werewolves: "the werewolf may have become extinct in our age, yet he has left his stamp on classical antiquity, he has trodden deep in Northern snows, has ridden rough-shod over the medievals, and has howled amongst Oriental sepulchres. ... Yet who knows! We may be a little too hasty in concluding that he is extinct."[170] However, Baring-Gould later attributes lycanthropy to the innate cruelty in humans, turning to examples of children and young boys "who assemble around a sheep or pig when it is about to be killed, and who watch the struggle of the dying brute with hearts

---

[169] Baring-Gould (in *The Book of Were-Wolves*) clearly states he was searching for a "real werewolf," saying, "I must acknowledge that I have been quite unsuccessful in obtaining a specimen of the animal," on page 7. One might be led to assume, judging from the direction his book later takes, that Baring-Gould became disgruntled in his fruitless search and decided that werewolves were madmen instead of ever possibly being a distinctive creature. Unlike Montague Summers, Baring-Gould not once entertains the notion of a human transforming into a wolf or wolf-man.

[170] Baring-Gould, *Book* 7

beating fast with pleasure, and eyes sparkling with delight."[171]

Baring-Gould's *The Book of Were-Wolves*, in his attempt to debunk werewolf legends, discusses extensively his own investigations into the human mind and general human behavior to eventually come to the conclusion that all madmen are, essentially, werewolves, and vice versa. He says "that children by nature are cruel, and that humanity has to be acquired by education."[172] Following many accounts of insanity and cannibalism, none of which remotely relate to werewolf legends, Baring-Gould makes the assertion that "[t]he cases in which bloodthirstiness and cannibalism are united with insanity are those which properly fall under the head of Lycanthropy."[173] However, Baring-Gould here does not use the proper idea of clinical lycanthropy, which is – in fact – a person having delusions of turning into a wolf or some other animal,[174]

---

[171] Baring-Gould, *Book* 56

[172] Baring-Gould, *Book* 57

[173] Baring-Gould, *Book* 61

[174] Garlipp 19. As mentioned throughout the article and defined in the opening sentence, although the word "lycanthropy" is derived from the Greek word for "wolf" (lykos), it can refer to a patient suffering delusions of being transformed into any kind of animal.

rather than anything specifically related to cannibalism or bloodthirstiness. Nonetheless, Baring-Gould decides that all of the cases he lists in Chapter IX of his book are instances of clinical lycanthropy, assuming that they "point unmistakably to hallucination,"[175] despite no account actually specifying this. Indeed, Baring-Gould seems so passionate in his determination to paint all werewolf legends as being nothing more than tales of madmen that he forgets an essential component of werewolf tales: a connection and usually a transformation into a wolf. In his texts, Baring-Gould essentially defines all individuals who suffer from insanity to be "lycanthropist[s],"[176] regardless of whether they exhibit any delusions related to wolves. Baring-Gould's writing expresses a frustration with the idea that anyone could ever believe a werewolf legend to be true, to the point that he not only attempts to debunk the myth by calling werewolves madmen, but also takes a much greater leap, saying that *all* madmen are werewolves – a sentiment not at all shared by those of the late

---

[175] Baring-Gould, *Book* 61

[176] Baring-Gould, *Book* 61

Middle Ages and the Early Modern period, but certainly an example of how, by the 1800s, scholars still felt the need to try to debunk werewolf legends and deal with locals who actually believed in them.

Likewise, throughout his book *Werewolf*, written in 1933, Montague Summers recounts many legends of locals believing in werewolves, even during the 1800s-1900s, and Summers himself believed in human transformation – while also dismissing the prospect of passing off lycanthropy as madness, saying that the term "werewolf" is often misused by other scholars to refer to madmen who have no connection with werewolves. In the 1600s, in Italy, werewolves were referred to as *lupo mannaro*, and they were actively feared as monsters.[177] The Italians of the Alpine provinces believed in demons who could "transform [themselves] into a wolf,"[178] further highlighting connections that the Church later asserted between werewolves and Satan. These demonic wolf

---

[177] Summers, *Werewolf* 162. *Lupo mannaro* literally means "werewolf," and it seems to be the only phrase in which these words are conjugated in such a way.

[178] Summers, *Werewolf* 162

shapeshifters were said to have an unquenchable thirst for blood, and werewolf scholar Montague Summers attests to having personally "met peasants who firmly believed in and dreaded the *lupo mannaro*," though he wrote his book *Werewolf* during the 1900s.[179] These *lupo mannaro* are but one of many examples of local werewolf legends that Summers details throughout his extensive and thorough research, even if he frequently injects his own biases.

In the introduction of his study, Summers mentions *The Book of Were-Wolves* by Sabine Baring-Gould, saying, "[H]e devotes no less than three chapters ... to a highly romantic and not very accurate account of Gilles de Rais, who was a Satanist certainly, but not a werewolf."[180] Summers even dismisses Baring-Gould's would-be scientific explanations of lycanthropy, calling his chapters on the subject

---

[179] Summers, *Werewolf* 162

[180] Summers, *Werewolf* xi. Summers also takes issue with Baring-Gould categorizing so many broad types of madmen and Satanists specifically as "werewolves," as was mentioned earlier in this chapter. I cannot wholly argue with all of those assertions, as Baring-Gould does go on quite a few tangents, though neither is Summers exactly perfect.

"unacceptable."[181] Indeed, Summers spends an entire paragraph in his introduction discussing that too many scholars do "not realize that werewolfery [is] a terrible and enduring fact,"[182] according to him. He says, in a very eloquent argument in favor of his theological (if, obviously, highly unconventional) point of view,

> I approach these problems entirely from the theological and philosophical point of view, where alone the solution can lie. Far be it from me to seem in any way to depreciate or underreckon the valuable work which has been done by anthropologists in collecting parallels from many countries and tracing significant rites and practice among primitive and distant folks, but they cannot read the riddle, and only too often have their guesses been far away from the truth. It could not be otherwise if they disregard the science of God for the science of man. Anthropology is but the humblest handmaid of theology.[183]

---

[181] Summers, *Werewolf* xi

[182] Summers, Werewolf xi

[183] Summers, *Werewolf* xii

However, despite his strong feelings regarding others who dismiss actual belief in werewolves, Summers acknowledges that the insane individuals whom other researchers refer to as "werewolves" are indeed madmen, but he claims the proper term for that insanity is "lycorexia or lycorrhexis,"[184] as lycanthropy is, at least to Summers, the *physical condition* of transforming into a wolf, not a form of insanity or delusion as claimed by those other researchers. Summers' writings emphasize the spiritual side of lycanthropy, but even so, he also emphasizes the evil within wolves and werewolves alike; essentially, Summers believes that werewolves are real, but they are created by Satanic magic.

---

[184] Summers, *Werewolf* 51. When he provides this definition, Summers is sympathetically detailing another werewolf court case, in 1852, in which a man went insane and believed he was transforming into a wolf. Summers describes the madman's death as "fearful mental agony, accusing himself of and being tortured by the guilt of heinous offences which he certainly had not committed. He died ... seemingly in the utmost spiritual dereliction. But this, we may hope, was the climax of his trial, for there appears little doubt from reading the details of the case that here we have a plain case of diabolical possession" (51), thus attributing this particular madman's insanity to possession rather than what Summers believes to be "true" lycanthropy (a physical transformation, not a delusional one).

The late 1500s and early 1600s became the ultimate transition period for lycanthropy: all traces of benevolence in werewolf legends were abolished by a combination of a greater, more connected combination of theology and science and law, and the very definition of a "werewolf" became confused. The rise of scientific thought and desire for rational explanations for all folkloric beliefs led to werewolves being designated as bloodthirsty madmen rather than anything more, and the theological nature of government and law at the time required the Church to respond, creating a combined answer to the issue that ultimately condemned werewolves from all legends. Beresford states it decently when he says that, during this time, the werewolf became little more than a "religious scapegoat,"[185] though this does not take into account a greater historic context: werewolves were not actually condemned by Christianity alone in the past, making them much more scapegoats of Early Modern science and law, which some scholars may think of only as religion at a surface-level examination. As if the already broad specifications – mostly put

---

[185] Beresford 88

in place later by scholars – that define a "werewolf" were not strange enough, during the late Middle Ages and the Early Modern period, werewolves became everything from sorcerers to madmen, some of whom did not even have delusions related to wolves. In the ancient era and the Middle Ages, lycanthropy was used in a variety of ways: it could be a morality lesson, often with the werewolf not even the individual at fault, or the werewolf in a story might be merely a person doing a favor for their traveling companions, or perhaps the werewolf was a noble knight or fearsome and respected berserker. However, during the late Middle Ages and the Early Modern period, werewolves transitioned into beings associated solely with evil, atrocities, and insanity: they were criminal madmen and Satanists of various sorts, condemned by the ruling governments of religion and science. Forgotten were the moral stories Christianity had previously used involving wolves and werewolves, such as *Bisclavret*, Giraldus Cambrensis's wolf that conversed with a priest, the wolf of Gubbio, and so many more. Due to the increasing influence of science and civilization's determination to "conquer" the wilderness, the ruling law ended any toleration of positive werewolf portrayals. During these time periods, werewolves and wolves became only symbols of evil and insanity, far more strongly and universally than they had been at any point in history. Such negative ideas of werewolves and wolves are only exaggerated further by today's scholars, who have so broadly labeled any case related to wolves as being a "werewolf trial," such as the many madmen discussed broadly by Baring-Gould, and especially the case of Peter Stubbe the sorcerer. Indeed, if any one account from the late Middle Ages and Early Modern period were to hold more power today than the rest, it would be that of Peter Stubbe, whose case as a sorcerer taking the form of a "strange and cruel wolf"[186] is full of elements never before associated with werewolves, in legend or even in other trial records of the same period. The labeling by modern scholars[187] of Peter Stubbe as a werewolf instead of a Satanist sorcerer – for he was

---

[186] "Stubbe" 73

[187] A reminder: Peter Stubbe was never called a "werewolf," "lycanthrope," or accused of "lycanthropy" in his own trial records, even in a time period in which courts believed in the existence of both werewolves and Satanic magic, and even in a connection between the two.

condemned as such: "a warning to all sorcerers and witches"[188] – is perhaps one of the single greatest reasons werewolves are still portrayed in such a negative light, even today. Thus, with werewolves becoming increasingly associated with Satanic transformations and illusions,[189] and many other werewolves summed up as simple but violent and cannibalistic madmen,[190] and modern scholars – influenced by our current popular culture – retroactively deeming so many of these cases to be werewolf legends regardless of the terminology of the time period, werewolves and wolves alike are left depicted as beings of utter malevolence, and these depictions are what the legendary werewolves, as well as their real and unsuspecting animal counterparts, unfortunately carried with them into the popular culture of the modern age.

---

[188] "Stubbe" 76

[189] A decent amount of this association also comes retroactively from modern scholarship, as mentioned previously with Peter Stubbe and certain others.

[190] At times, even including madmen lacking in any kind of wolfish symptoms or delusions, making any possible connection with werewolves questionable, to say the least.

Chapter IV – The Moon Waxes: The Werewolf Popularity Surge

Werewolves have held a place in fiction throughout human history, but in the past, the average person most likely believed in *real* werewolves as well as the fictional ones they read about in tales such as Marie de France's *Bisclavret*.[191] Today, the average consumers of popular culture have particular images and biases in mind when they hear or read the word "werewolf," particularly based on whatever work of entertainment first introduced them to the concept of lycanthropy – but that concept almost always involves either malevolence, or, at the very least, the werewolf in question becoming an uncontrollable beast when they transform. Although werewolves today come in a wide variety when examined on the surface, the concept of the werewolf has, at the same time, become more generalized and more confused. On average, when one examines any werewolf from popular culture, the werewolf will probably be uncontrollable when transformed or at least be prone to bloodthirsty rages and

---

[191] As covered in Chapter II of this study.

nearly always be associated in some fashion with either the moon or nightfall (this is not counting the obvious werewolf stories that largely spurn the moniker of "werewolf" due to these associations: the "wolf shifter" subgenre). Almost paradoxically, however, the concept of a werewolf has also become more confusing in that many artists and public commentators today add their own elements to werewolves or else take elements from past popular culture, ignoring any relation to legends. Most werewolves today are sensitive to silver, or belladonna or wolfsbane, and some even take elements from vampires and the undead in that they cannot cross running water, among other strange contrivances made in order to provide the werewolves of the story with some kind of "weakness" not present in any original folklore. In legends of the past, however, the idea of the werewolf – despite belief in the werewolf being a universal cultural phenomenon, spanning multiple continents and civilizations – feels more cohesive than today's conception, in which werewolves have gone from a feared monster to a bit of popular culture upon which all writers attempt to put their unique stamp, often with flagrant disregard to and ignorance of any legends. Regardless of how individual creators splice together their "unique" werewolf from their own ideas and concepts taken from other folkloric creatures never before associated with werewolves, however, one overarching element remains from the late Middle Ages and the Early Modern period: the werewolf, like its wolf counterpart, is still associated with malevolence and, more often than not, madness.

During the 1800s and early 1900s, werewolves were still what one might consider relatively unusual in entertainment, though a few notable stories included a single werewolf villain. In 1896, Clemence Housman published her first novel, *The Were-wolf*, an allegory about Christianity in which the devilish antagonist is a sexually obsessed seductress werewolf who lures men before she transforms into a werewolf to eat them, which seems to take a page from the rapacious sorcerer Peter Stubbe rather than any traditional werewolf legend.[192] Many

---

[192] As covered in Chapter III of this study, werewolves were never associated with sexual criminality and lust until the trial record of Peter Stubbe, who was actually tried as a sorcerer and not a werewolf, only to later be labeled a werewolf by scholars.

other examples of werewolf fiction exist from the 1800s, such as G.W.M. Reynolds's *Wagner the Wehr-Wolf* from 1847, in which the werewolf is the result of a deal with Satan. One could argue that Robert Louis Stevenson's timeless *Strange Case of Dr. Jekyll and Mr. Hyde*, published in 1886, is a werewolf story, but there is no direct mention of werewolves in the novel itself, despite the themes being easily translatable to a werewolf. However, *Dr. Jekyll and Mr. Hyde* boasts far more appeal and renown than any werewolf story from this period – or, indeed, the overwhelming majority of werewolf fiction yet told. One novel that received a fair amount of praise was Guy Endore's 1933 novel *The Werewolf of Paris*, which was later adapted into a film; however, *The Werewolf of Paris* provides yet another example of stories that turn werewolves into other legendary monsters, particularly since the predictably malevolent werewolf of *The Werewolf of Paris* must suck the blood of a woman in order to aid in resisting his transformations, similar to some sort of vampire.

Although several films from previous periods featured werewolves, such as *The Werewolf* in 1913 and *Wolf Blood* in 1925,

MAEGAN A. STEBBINS

and the first werewolf movie of the sound era was *Werewolf of London* in 1935, the single most influential piece of popular culture upon the modern concept of werewolves today is undoubtedly *The Wolf Man* (1941), starring Lon Chaney, Jr. Though werewolves have never enjoyed considerable and high-quality attention in mainstream media, even with the increase they have seen today (which will be discussed later in this chapter), there has never been any work, legendary or fictional, to exert so much influence over the societal idea of a werewolf as did this film. Put simply, *The Wolf Man* created the imagery, general storyline, character, and lore that are still so closely associated with the werewolf today. Werewolves still haunt the dark, Gothic architecture and haunted forests seen in the film, and many werewolf stories still tell the same general tale of someone being "infected" with lycanthropy, transforming, and eventually meeting some kind of tragic and occasionally ironic death.[193] Likewise, the character of Larry Talbot still survives

---

[193] In Talbot's case, he is bludgeoned to death by his own father, using the silver head of his walking stick. Almost every other movie werewolf faces similar fates, and it is undeniable that – especially in film – the werewolf is nearly always killed.

today in much werewolf fiction: a nice and sympathetic character who must somehow attempt to cope with his monstrous and uncontrollable transformations, and in the end, the curse results in his death.

Of all the ways in which *The Wolf Man* so heavily influenced werewolves in popular culture today, perhaps the greatest contribution the film made to the modern concept of werewolves is the idea of silver as being the werewolf's one true weakness. The film writer Curt Siodmak created this entire concept on his own, instead of drawing it from legend,[194] and yet most people today accept it as truth that werewolves should

---

[194] Silver being a werewolf's weakness is sometimes wrongfully attributed to legend, but before *The Wolf Man*, werewolves were never connected to silver in any way. Silver was occasionally, but rarely, mentioned to ward off witches and sorcerers – but, again, as we have seen, those were not werewolves. Some authors, such as Brad Steiger and Robert Jackson, claim that the idea of silver killing werewolves originates with the legend of the Beast of Gévaudan, but they cite no reliable sources and their research seems very insufficient to back this claim. The most often-cited source is actually a fictional novel published in 1946, which is after the release of *The Wolf Man*, and the book is Henri Pourrat's *Historie fidèle de la bête en Gévaudan*. Likewise, it is extremely arguable whether the Beast of Gévaudan should be considered a werewolf legend at all, and a case could very easily be made against ever citing it as a werewolf legend.

be sensitive to silver, even if a few of the most modern werewolf stories are now attempting to shed this concept.[195] As seen in legend, werewolves have no real "weaknesses," and particularly not any that apply across nearly all their legends, as do most portrayals of vampires, making Siodmak's contribution significant to modern werewolf portrayals. Silver as a werewolf's weakness has infiltrated popular culture so deeply that there now exist sayings about using a "silver bullet" when discussing something with only one weakness, almost like an "Achilles heel." Likewise, other elements of the film have come to be generally accepted as the "proper" or "normal" portrayal of a werewolf, such as how the lycanthrope undergoes transformations into a werewolf against his will after being bitten by another werewolf, turning lycanthropy into more of a rabies-like disease rather than a curse: yet another shift toward depicting werewolves as afflicted madmen. The werewolf

---

[195] I feel the need to note that I personally do enjoy the silver concept, and I use it in my own fiction. My words and arguments are not a slight against the narrative tool as a whole, but I must point out how it is not folkloric. In fact, I use many narrative tools I may sound negative about in this book, as I think they can be used well and tell a good story.

transforming at the full moon, however, was actually popularized by the film's sequel, *Frankenstein Meets the Wolf Man* (1943), in which the film's famous rhyme was altered to specify the transformation as occurring "when the moon is full and bright," instead of "when the wolfbane blooms and the autumn moon is bright." Therefore, *The Wolf Man*'s many contributions to the modern concept of werewolves, especially giving them silver as their only weakness and transferring the curse by bite, makes the film stand tall among other werewolf fiction as almost certainly the single most influential werewolf story ever conceived.

Another very influential werewolf story took the form of a television show instead of a movie, when the Gothic soap opera *Dark Shadows* aired on ABC from 1966 to 1971. Although werewolves and vampires have sometimes been associated in legend, such as the vrykolakas in Greece and Eastern Europe, they had never appeared together as the headline monsters in a story – or, at least, not a popular one with wide appeal – until *Dark Shadows*, which starred many assorted monsters, including most prominently vampires, werewolves, and witches. It took many long years for the idea of vampires and werewolves existing in the same setting to take hold, but very recently, the idea has captivated audiences, and today, one is almost never found without the other, though they are generally portrayed as rivals, as will be seen in some examples featured later in this chapter.[196]

After *The Wolf Man* and the various sequels it spawned, other werewolf movies were created, though none were terribly influential or popular. It was not until the 1980s that

---

[196] There are innumerable examples from modern fiction, such as the *World of Darkness* setting. A notable and unfortunate example is the immensely popular, even in the eyes of the average consumer, *Underworld* film series, which features vampires and werewolves (or "lycans," as the series calls them) at eternal war. However, there has never been a true werewolf hero in the *Underworld* series, as the vampire protagonist played by Kate Beckinsale only slays both vampire and werewolf villains (the latter generally portrayed as incredibly unthreatening to the vampire heroine), despite werewolves being cast as theoretically sympathetic in the setting of the films, since they were supposedly created by the vampires as a slave race. Expansion upon *Underworld* and its werewolves could be made, but the films are overall an unremarkable stain upon werewolves in popular culture save for incredible contributions in the field of werewolf design and practical film effects, and to dedicate too much discussion to that series and its narratives would ultimately degrade this study as a whole.

werewolves saw another revival of sorts, which also took place in film. *The Howling* and *An American Werewolf in London*, both released in 1981, became prominent werewolf fiction of the modern era, with both predictably casting werewolves as irredeemable villains. In the case of *The Howling*, the movie varies the typical plot that werewolf movies largely retell from *The Wolf Man*, and instead the movie is about an entire mountain resort occupied by werewolves; however, true to the form popularized by *The Wolf Man*, the protagonist of the film is still "infected"[197] with lycanthropy and is killed in the conclusion of the movie; *The Howling* also makes the very unfortunate addition of emphasizing sex with the werewolves, in the spirit of Peter Stubbe. *An American Werewolf in London*, however, tells a tale almost exactly like *The Wolf Man*: an innocent man, in this case a tourist, is infected with lycanthropy and eventually dies tragically, with his lover watching. However, *An American Werewolf in London* makes

---

[197] Note again the emphasis on "infection" in modern werewolf media, away from the magical curse of older folklore. This also ties to the Early Modern conception of werewolves in relation to insanity and disease.

strange alterations to the idea of the werewolf in the film, as the werewolf is haunted by the visages of the people he has killed, who insist he must commit suicide. It also represents one of the earliest popular ironic and rather self-aware portrayals of werewolves: a concept that has, unfortunately, gained enormous popularity.

Another noteworthy film in terms of werewolf popularity is the 1985 comedy film *Teen Wolf*, starring Michael J. Fox. Unlike horror movies focusing on werewolves, *Teen Wolf* portrays werewolves as unfortunately comical, being a comedy, but they are not necessarily malevolent. However, when the protagonist begins to transform into a werewolf, his father (also a werewolf) warns him not to lose his temper. Although the werewolves in the movie retain full control of themselves when transformed, and indeed the protagonist uses his lycanthropy to gain popularity within the school instead of being shunned as he originally fears he will be, they are nonetheless dangerous due to their powerful animalistic nature. *Teen Wolf* actually harkens back to some of the oldest werewolf legends (although it almost certainly does not do this on purpose), in that the werewolf, as a motif, is used to help tell a moral story about acceptance, self-discovery, self-control, and simply being different.[198]

Many other werewolf movies have been created, largely inspired by *The Wolf Man*, and a complete list of werewolf films would be long and tedious – but most of them share a stigma in common: comical or not, not only is the werewolf usually malevolent, but also, werewolf movies are generally considered B-list films that do not receive much recognition or popularity, usually rightfully so due to poorly written stories and equally poor production values. Whenever a film is branded as a "werewolf movie," it often results in audiences preemptively judging the film to be rather silly and most likely predictable and stereotypical horror, which essentially follows the plot set

---

[198] Another important aspect to many of the werewolf films of the 1980s is that they are dark comedies or openly lighthearted comedies, and they set the trend for many decades to come. Much as Hollywood has done with many fantastical creatures and story elements, werewolves have – by and large – been tragically condemned today to either be simplistic horror monsters as discussed throughout this study, or else they are simply a joke. The endless barrage of comedic werewolf fiction creates a vast hinderance upon any progression toward meaningful stories about werewolves. Creators, likewise, are essentially told that werewolves cannot be taken seriously by modern audiences.

by *The Wolf Man* in the 40s or some other horror story. For instance, a typical werewolf movie (when it is not simply using the same basic plot of *The Wolf Man*) may be along the lines of survival horror films, like *Dog Soldiers* (2002), a film – again, with many comedic elements, despite its dark nature – in which a squad of soldiers must survive an attack by bloodthirsty werewolves. Like so many werewolf movies before it, *Dog Soldiers* has helped werewolf films maintain their stigma of being celebrations of gore (and, frequently, sex, again defying more traditional werewolf tales in favor of depicting werewolves as stereotypical malevolent horror figures), with the various characters killed in assorted shocking ways destined to garner strong audience reactions. Due to their usually very simple nature and even simpler stories, which are often crude and centered around little more than violence and sex, werewolf movies have, as a genre, embraced rather than combatted the stigma of being low-quality, forgettable horror flicks, turning the werewolf into a cheesy and dislikable trope that often self-referentially teases and openly degrades itself, building upon the average consumer's refusal and borderline inability to take them seriously. In film, werewolves are – even today – almost always solely malevolent in purpose and nature, and their characters are drawn far more often from sorcerous madmen like Peter Stubbe than from the werewolf of legend.

In past entertainment depictions, werewolves appeared with varied motives across different mediums, although they were still shrouded in obscurity, with the term "werewolf" usually taken to indicate a frivolous, cheap production, despite the potential quality of the story. A prime example of this stigma is found in *Captain America* comic book issues #402-#408, entitled the "Man And Wolf" story arc, first published in 1992. In this storyline, Steve Rogers (Captain America) must contend with werewolves that appear, at first, to be villainous, until he uncovers a dangerous plot – while, at the same time, turning into a werewolf, himself. Though sometimes harshly criticized by comic book fans, the "Capwolf" comics tell a robust and interesting story, with well-drawn artwork accurately depicting wolf posture and interesting explorations into various characters and the lore of the Marvel universe, particularly where werewolves and their varieties are concerned. A likely reason for the derision of the comic series is simply that the association with werewolves makes it seem B-list and silly, although the comics do an excellent job tying together and telling a story about the various kinds of werewolves and werewolf-like beings and mutants in Marvel, and Steve Rogers proves himself to be so interesting and effective as a werewolf that he exhibits werewolf transformations and powers in later comics, with some depictions of Capwolf persisting today, though modern depictions are much more in the vein of self-referential dog-joke material. Despite their obscurity and the criticism from some comic fans, the original *Captain America* "Man And Wolf" storyline stands out as an excellent depiction of werewolves, particularly those of a benevolent nature, most notably that of Captain America himself, which shows that werewolves need not always be portrayed as one-sidedly malevolent.

Though werewolves have occasionally appeared in popular media, they have yet to be the primary focus of a popular and successful story, but they have assumed minor roles in other fantasy and paranormal works, such as the *Harry Potter* novel series. Although werewolves never take a prominent role, some important supporting characters in the

Harry Potter series are werewolves, most notably Professor Remus Lupin. Throughout the *Harry Potter* series, starting with *Harry Potter and the Prisoner of Azkaban*, Lupin proves himself to be among the kindest, humblest, and most helpful of all the characters, particularly among the professors at Hogwarts, though he himself does not exhibit any particularly memorable character traits other than his lycanthropy. However, even the protagonists of the novel react violently and with great fear upon learning he is a werewolf. Lupin later transforms and turns against his friends, though he ultimately runs off without doing them considerable harm; however, in the books, he is nonetheless a considerable and terrifying threat, even to Buckbeak the hippogriff.[199] Therefore, Lupin's benevolence as a character exists only while he remains in his human form, for if he transforms into a werewolf (unless he takes a special potion that allows him to control himself), he becomes a

---

[199] This was depicted very poorly and inaccurately to the novel, in so many ways, in the film adaptation of *The Prisoner of Azkaban*. Indeed, the film adaptations of all the books instead predictably cast werewolves in a much less powerful, much more dismissive, and sometimes outright comical light, more in tune with the average werewolf media and unlike the novels themselves.

malevolent and destructive monster. Other werewolves are mentioned broadly multiple times throughout the *Harry Potter* series, even if only in passing, and they are generally regarded with disdain and suspicion, particularly as characters in later installments of the series shun those who have werewolf friends.[200] Regardless of the sympathetic nature of Lupin, werewolves are still largely considered malevolent in the *Harry Potter* series, even though they are occasionally used as a means of representing misunderstood and marginalized minorities in society. Most werewolves are said to work with Lord Voldemort, the primary antagonist, and one of the later villains is a mad and bloodthirsty werewolf named Fenrir Greyback. Overall, though Lupin is a modern instance of a sympathetic werewolf, he is nonetheless uncontrollable and his wolf side is malevolent, and werewolves as creatures in the setting are evil and destructive. In spite of this, however, the *Harry Potter* series handles its werewolf lore far better than much modern media, with good sympathetic portrayals and interesting characters

---

[200] There are several instances in *Harry Potter and the Goblet of Fire* in which characters criticize Harry Potter for having once made friends with a werewolf (Lupin).

carrying internal conflict.

Perhaps the greatest popularity surge werewolves have seen thus far, which still survives even now in 2017, occurred with the release of the *Twilight* novel series. Even though the werewolves in the series are unusual and many people attempted to turn werewolves into a laughing stock due to their role in the series, the overall success of the books undeniably resulted in an increase of interest in werewolves of all kinds. In the first installment of the series, *Twilight*, the werewolf character Jacob Black indicates that he and his ancestors are werewolves, and he calls them such, even though he says they are wolves that turn into humans, instead of vice versa. This is referenced in *New Moon* when Bella realizes what Jacob really is: *"You see, the cold ones are the natural enemies of the wolf—well, not the wolf really, but the wolves that turn into men, like our ancestors. You would call them werewolves."*[201] Likewise, in *New Moon*, the first novel in the series to portray werewolves instead of merely mentioning them, when Bella initially figures out that Jacob is a werewolf, she thinks, "I didn't know anything

---

[201] Meyer, *New Moon* 293

about werewolves, clearly. I would have expected something closer to the movies—big, hairy half-men creatures or something—if I'd expected anything at all,"[202] making reference specifically to the way the werewolves of the *Twilight* series turn into giant wolves, rather than the humanoid werewolf arguably more common to popular culture. The series also emphasizes that werewolves and vampires have a rivalry and have been enemies for many ages, as stated by Jacob; ever since *Dark Shadows* combined werewolves and vampires, it has become popular to turn them into rivals (which has no roots in legend), and the popularity of *Twilight* only aided in solidifying this idea throughout the series. Regardless, the werewolves in *Twilight*, while they are said to have violent tempers, still retain control of themselves and are generally portrayed in a positive light, at least in *New Moon*.

However, despite being called werewolves throughout the book, the werewolves in *New Moon* are also identified as "Quileutes,"[203] and the fourth installment in the series, *Breaking*

---

[202] Meyer, *New Moon* 298

[203] Meyer, *New Moon* 386

Dawn, changes the idea of *Twilight's* benevolent werewolves. For whatever reason, in *Breaking Dawn*, Stephenie Meyer decided that her self-controlled werewolves were not actually "true" werewolves at all. *Breaking Dawn* specifies that the Quileutes, like Jacob and his pack, are shape-shifters, not true werewolves, which would mean that "true werewolves" are to be depicted as mad and uncontrollable, thus undoubtedly at least somewhat malevolent in nature as a result. This clarification comes, oddly, at the very end of the final book in the series, when Edward tells another vampire that the shape-shifters called "werewolves" throughout the series so far "'aren't even werewolves.'"[204] Though there is no clarification

---

[204] Meyer, *Breaking Dawn* 704. At this point in the series, and after calling them "werewolves" for so long, it seems odd for Meyer to suddenly decide that the fact that they are wolf shape-shifters is sheer coincidence, instead of holding any significance regarding their being werewolves, the ancient enemies of the vampires. Apparently, however, the true werewolves of the *Twilight* series are actually far more powerful and intimidating than are the shape-shifters, which is at least an interesting change from many other forms of media featuring vampire and werewolf rivalries, in which the vampires are often more powerful – although the vampires in *Twilight* have, despite the supposed power of the werewolves, somehow managed to hunt true werewolves to the verge of extinction.

regarding whether the "true" werewolves, the Children of the Moon, are malevolent or not in nature, it is specified that the shape-shifters like Jacob "think of themselves as werewolves, [but] they are not. The more accurate name for them would be shape-shifters. The choice of a wolf form was purely by chance. ... These creatures have nothing to do with the Children of the Moon. They have merely inherited this skill from their fathers. It's genetic—they do not continue their species by infecting others the way true werewolves do."[205] Apparently, in the *Twilight* series, the vampires – specifically, one named Caius – had hunted werewolves almost to extinction, again popularizing the idea of werewolves and vampires as ancient rivals. When Bella asks about the werewolves, Edward clarifies, "'Full moon, yes, ... Silver bullets, no—that was just another one of those myths to make humans feel like they had a sporting chance.'"[206] He also mentions that true werewolves, "rarely

---

[205] Meyer, *Breaking Dawn* 704-705. Again, note the emphasis on "infection" in relation to the "true werewolves," much more a callback to modern media than to the cursed werewolves and/or shapeshifters of legend. In a way, Jacob's pack has more in common with folkloric werewolves than do these Children of the Moon.

[206] Meyer, Breaking Dawn 745

move in packs, and they are never much in control of themselves."[207] Although the *Twilight* series does subvert most modern werewolves by making them not sensitive to silver, the differences between the *Twilight* werewolves and more typical modern werewolves become lessened by the odd distinction between the shape-shifters and the "true" werewolves.

The *Twilight* series resulted in a considerable resurgence of interest in werewolves, inspiring many different werewolf stories: some continued the same werewolf horror trend, while others picked up on *Twilight's* more unconventional portrayal of werewolves and vampires, and lycanthropes and the concept of "werewolf packs" began to appear more frequently in teenage romance. One of the most successful teen paranormal romances – and one of the few to focus exclusively on werewolves instead of vampires, along with a number of other supernatural beings – is the MTV television show *Teen Wolf*, which began its run in 2011 and is due to conclude mid-2017. Although the series is named after the 1985 comedy film previously mentioned, there are few

---

[207] Meyer, Breaking Dawn 745

similarities. Unlike its namesake film, the *Teen Wolf* series portrays werewolves as uncontrollable and dangerous, particularly in the first season, which also features a werewolf as the main antagonist. However, obviously, werewolves are largely portrayed as sympathetic throughout the show, and ultimately, the *Teen Wolf* television show represents one of the latest installments in a small but possibly growing trend of stories portraying werewolves as sympathetic and sometimes benevolent, even if this trend is still largely confined to the paranormal romance genre.

The success of books such as *Harry Potter* and *Twilight* has led to similar tales of magic with monstrous elements, and one can find both werewolves and wolves depicted in a variety of young-adult fiction today. They are, however, still generally cast as villains, and even if there are a few reasonably "good" and/or sympathetic exceptions, the "race" of wolves or werewolves are often evil as a whole, with only a few fairly recent young-adult novels starting to alter this trope. Unfortunately, such novels often go under the radar for "mainstream" popular culture, such as those books that become popular films and so deeply ingrain themselves in the common mind of society.[208] One exception to malevolent werewolves appears in Neil Gaiman's *The Graveyard Book*, which is essentially a Gothic retelling of Rudyard Kipling's *The Jungle Book*, using ghosts, vampires, and werewolves instead of the various jungle animals. Like Lupin in the *Harry Potter* series, the werewolf in *The Graveyard Book* also has prematurely greying hair and an obviously wolfish name, the former of which is a strange aspect contrived by modern popular culture that has become quite common: "Miss Lupescu was not pretty. Her face was pinched and her expression was disapproving. Her hair was grey, although her face seemed too young for grey hair."[209] However, Gaiman's story takes an unexpected turn when the nature of the werewolves in *The Graveyard Book* is revealed to be

---

[208] This has primarily come in the form of good or sympathetic wolves, as opposed to werewolves. Examples of fairly recent works featuring sympathetic wolves include *The Cry of the Wolf* by Melvin Burgess, written in 1990; *The True Story of the Three Little Pigs* by Jon Scieszka and Lane Smith, written in 1989; and a picture book *The Three Little Wolves and the Big Bad Pig* by Eugene Trivizas and illustrated by Helen Oxenbury, published in 1993. Unfortunately, books such as these have not achieved exceptional popularity, even while receiving recognition through awards. Regardless, stories such as these are a decent start to reversing the negativity of wolf portrayals.

[209] Gaiman 66

benevolent. When Bod, the protagonist, first sees the werewolf, he believes it to be an evil monster planning to eat him, but it is actually Miss Lupescu descending into Hell to rescue him from being kidnapped. Later, he learns: *"Those that men call Werewolves or Lycanthropes call themselves the Hounds of God, as they claim their transformation is a gift from their creator, and they repay the gift with their tenacity, for they will pursue an evildoer to the very gates of Hell."*[210] Although Miss Lupescu meets the usual fate of the werewolf when she is killed, Gaiman subverts traditional popular culture by drawing from Thies's trial[211] to portray werewolves as benevolent, serving God rather than the Devil.

Werewolves have also made numerous appearances in video games throughout the existence of the medium, dating back to *Altered Beast* in 1988 and several video games before it. In recent years, however, werewolves have become more prominent in some very popular video games. The player character has been able to become a werewolf in nearly every installment of the *Elder Scrolls* series, most prominently

---

[210] Gaiman 97

[211] As discussed in Chapter III of this study.

including the second expansion pack to *Elder Scrolls III*, *Bloodmoon*, which released in 2003 and focuses entirely on werewolves and Hircine, the largely evil being who created and controls them. In *Bloodmoon*, if the player becomes a werewolf, they must devour the corpse of a humanoid NPC[212] every night or be considerably weakened. *The Elder Scrolls* series skipped over werewolves in the fourth installment, *Oblivion*, but brought back playable werewolves in *The Elder Scrolls V: Skyrim*, though the system for werewolves is far less robust than it was in *Bloodmoon*. Likewise, werewolves have appeared as a playable race or class in many other video games, mostly medieval fantasy RPGs,[213] such as the Druid class in *Diablo II* (2000), and the Druid Shapeshifter class in *Baldur's Gate II: Shadows of Amn* and its expansion pack, *Throne of Bhaal*. In both *Diablo* and *Baldur's Gate*, the transformation of the player into a werewolf is a class ability that has no effect on how other characters in

---

[212] Non-Player Character

[213] Role-Playing Games. Trying to truly define "what is a RPG" is a long-standing argument that will not be addressed here. Needless to say, the games mentioned are all considered by someone to be RPGs in some way or another, regardless of how true the definition may be in some cases.

the game react to the player, unlike *Bloodmoon,* in which the world will turn hostile to the player if their lycanthropy is ever discovered. One of the latest major games to include werewolves is *World of Warcraft* (originally released in 2004), the most successful MMORPG[214] ever created. In 2010, Blizzard – the company that develops *World of Warcraft* – released the expansion pack *Cataclysm,* which added the "worgen" (the setting's term for werewolves) as a playable race, including the ability to cosmetically shapeshift between human and werewolf forms.[215] These are, however, only the select few games that let the player become a werewolf – in the majority of video games that include werewolves, they are simply evil monsters that will attack the player on sight and must be killed, often without much – if any – story or fanfare.

Just as werewolves appear in every other form of media, from movies and television shows to books and comics, and even to video games, lycanthropes have long had a place in music, particularly various genres of rock and metal.

---

[214] Massively Multiplayer Online Role-Playing Game

[215] Though it is noteworthy that, tragically, the worgen have always been snubbed by the developers in a wide variety of ways.

"Werewolves of London" by Warren Zevon may be among the best-known of werewolf songs, and it largely portrays werewolves in a comical – if violent and rapacious – sense, even while referencing several werewolf horror movies, and indeed the song may very well be using "werewolf" as a metaphor entirely. However, most werewolf songs continue the trend of associating werewolves with violence and madness, with few exceptions. For instance, the music video for Disturbed's werewolf song "The Animal," the lyrics of which discuss transforming under the moonlight and losing control to become a beast personifying Death, portrays what looks like Satanic ritual, and the lyrics include "we both shall dine in Hell tonight."[216] Metallica's "Of Wolf and Man" actually portrays lycanthropy as a positive state, implying its oneness with nature, in both the refrain, "Earth's gift, back to the meaning of life," and the bridge, "Wildness is the preservation of the world / So seek the wolf in thyself."[217] However, the werewolf's association with negativity, madness, and nightmare is so

---

[216] Draiman

[217] Hetfield

powerful today that it leaves audiences calling many songs "werewolf songs," even if the songs in question do not overtly mention wolves or werewolves at all, such as "Monster" by Skillet, the refrain of which includes "I hate what I've become, the nightmare's just begun / I must confess that I feel like a monster."[218] Likewise, another popular werewolf song with no mention of wolves or werewolves is "Animal I Have Become" by Three Days Grace, with notable nightmare lyrics such as, "Somebody wake me from this nightmare / I can't escape this hell."[219]

The modern idea of a werewolf, then, is perhaps exemplified in the dark description offered by Stephen Jones, who compiled many werewolf and shapeshifter short stories (all horror, with the overwhelming majority portraying werewolves as irredeemable, sexually driven beings of evil) in his *Mammoth Book of Wolf Men*. Jones defines werewolves as follows: "Condemned (usually through no fault of their own) to metamorphose during the phases of the full moon into bestial

---

[218] Cooper

[219] Gontier

killers who destroy the ones they love, werewolves exemplify the classic dichotomy of Good versus Evil which ... lies at the core of most great modern horror fiction."[220] Clearly, Jones defines the modern concept of lycanthropy, which, when put into perspective, appears alarmingly different from the classical, mythological conceptions of werewolves, even if werewolves of legend were also sometimes cursed to transform under certain conditions and timeframes. Jones describes the werewolf as constituting the conflict of "good versus evil." This idea is strange, particularly given that malevolent werewolves of legend were evil in *both* forms, more often than not. Werewolves have, over time, taken a new shape in the mind of modern audiences, with the tragic result being that the wolf in the werewolf is used only to portray incredible evil. Further highlighting the strange modern idea of a werewolf, Jones concludes the introduction of his short story collection with the statement, "[G]et your silver bullets ready as the sign of the pentagram reveals the Beast that lurks within the heart of

---

[220] Jones xii

Man."[221] By referring to silver and a relation to the pentagram (which is now considered a symbol of Satanism, with which the werewolf today has been associated since the court cases of the late Middle Ages and Early Modern period[222]), Jones is referencing only aspects of werewolves that originated in in *The Wolf Man*.

These examples and countless others of werewolves in entertainment across all forms of media – including many not covered here, such as card games, board games, and more – serve to highlight the fact that many werewolves are portrayed as malevolent. Today, popular culture has latched onto many ideas established by the writer of *The Wolf Man* (1941), Curt Siodmak, who portrayed the werewolf as a beast defeated only by silver, who transforms at a particular time of the year (established to be the full moon in *Frankenstein Meets the Wolf Man* [1943]), and whose transformations result in his becoming a demonically-inspired monster driven solely by the need to kill humans.[223] Indeed, modern werewolf fiction frequently

---

[221] Jones xiii

[222] As covered in Chapter III of this study.

[223] In the film, the werewolf sees a pentagram on his next victim's

equates the werewolf side of lycanthropes with the Devil, the purest form of evil, an idea which has survived over the centuries into today from the trials of sorcerers and madmen of the late Middle Ages and Early Modern period, rather than from the many werewolf legends throughout history. Thus, although werewolves are still relatively popular today and have seen a popularity surge with *Twilight*, they are nonetheless far more often portrayed as villains. Even when they are sympathetic, they are still generally considered uncontrollable, man-eating monsters, with often the most benign or benevolent (in human form) of them featured as secondary characters, who are killed by the end of the story. Surely now is the time for such an overwhelmingly negative portrayal of werewolves and wolves to change: not only are modern storytellers casting aside the deepest roots of the werewolf legend by always casting werewolves as villains – leading to

---

skin. This was another contrivance created by Curt Siodmak, which has no foundation in folklore. Although the association between werewolves and pentagrams did not take nearly as powerful a hold on popular culture as did the idea of a werewolf being sensitive to silver, it is still noteworthy that any association found between the two today originated from the film, not anywhere else.

inaccurate assumptions and ignorance of many powerful legends in the history of numerous cultures around the world – but also these powerfully negative and destructive portrayals condemn a *real* animal: the wolf.

THE WEREWOLF: PAST AND FUTURE

Chapter V – The Benefits of Reintroducing the Benevolent Werewolf

As shown throughout this study, werewolves and wolves have been portrayed in various ways by cultures around the world over the course of history; in ages past, they were frequently seen as benevolent or at least neutral, but with the rise of civilization conquering wilderness, the advent of scientific rationale for legends, and a widespread law enforcement based in the aforementioned science over folk beliefs, the cultures that once revered the wolf as a brother and a mentor increasingly portrayed werewolves and wolves as madmen. By the late Middle Ages and into the Early Modern period, werewolves and wolves were believed to be beings of pure evil. These beliefs carried into the modern age, and they have never left us – today, the fictional werewolves and real wolves exist under an irrational stigma of malevolence, along with various negative characteristics that have been unreasonably attributed to them over the course of history: ruthlessness, gluttony, greed, selfishness, madness,

137

sometimes outright stupidity, and, now, even sexual obsession and predation. For many ages, and for the entirety of the modern period, werewolves and wolves have suffered under these negative portrayals, but it is time for these perceptions to change. Casting werewolves solely as villains, modern storytellers dismiss or do not bother discovering the ancient roots of the werewolf legend, leading to inaccurate assumptions and ignorance of an array of myths both powerful and moral that exist across many cultures around the world. This depiction comes with extreme irony, in that wolves are considered villains for many attributes that other animals would theoretically represent far more efficiently, and wolves' many very positive behaviors are ignored entirely. Now that scientists have had the means and opportunity to examine animals so closely, it is hardly justice to portray male lions as symbols of great nobility and mercy, while condemning wolves to be symbols of selfishness and evil – but these trends continue due to ignorance and unwillingness to change from classical conceptions, and this is merely one example of many such undue biases.[224] The depiction of werewolves and wolves as malevolent has resulted in negative consequences, such as ignorance of historical legends, as well as extinction, endangerment, cruel methods of hunting, and general misunderstanding and hatred of real wolves: a hatred that mankind still refuses to leave behind, even today.

Unlike so many other animals – most notably other mammals, such as lions and bears – wolves have always suffered from a stigma of negativity, being cast as villains in everything from fairytales to modern-day children's cartoons, and this is due in no small part to the relatively recent determination to always depict the wolves' fictional half-human counterparts, werewolves, as evil. As stated by Barry Lopez in his book *Of Wolves and Men*, "The wolf exerts a powerful influence on the human imagination. It takes your

---

[224] As stated by Otten in the Introduction of *A Lycanthropy Reader*, on page 2, "The irony [of depicting werewolves and wolves as pure evil] is that animal wolves (except in case of injury or hunger) do not kill, attack, or mutilate. According to recent research, wolves live in packs and establish congenial, bonding relationships and a society founded on trust. If one of their number develops killer-instincts, that criminal wolf is destroyed for the good of the community."

stare and turns it back on you. (The Bella Coola Indians believed that someone once tried to change all the animals into men but succeeded in making human only the eyes of the wolf.) ... Wolf-haters want to say they are born killers, which isn't true."[225] For many ages, wolves have appeared in a variety of stories, and they feature perhaps most prominently in fairytales.

The wolf in fairytales is almost always portrayed as a villain and a kind of personification of gluttony, particularly given his insistence upon swallowing everything (and everyone) whole, such as in perhaps the most famous of wolf fairytales, "Little Red Riding Hood." Although the tale has been told many times and in many ways, the original story did not have quite the happy ending that it often does today: instead, the wolf eats Little Red Riding Hood, and that is the end of the story: "Upon saying these words, the wicked wolf threw himself on Little Red Riding Hood and gobbled her up."[226] Perrault, from whom we receive perhaps the oldest version of this tale,

---

[225] Lopez 4

[226] Perrault 13

then reminds the reader of the story's moral, saying that girls should not "listen to just anyone,"[227] or they may be eaten by a wolf. Notably, Perrault adds that "I say a wolf, but not all wolves / Are exactly the same. / Some are perfectly charming, / Not loud, brutal, or angry, / But tame, pleasant, and gentle, / ... But watch out if you haven't learned that tame wolves / Are the most dangerous of all."[228] Clearly, Perrault is using the wolf to represent a malicious and rapacious individual – and he chooses a wolf because, unfortunately, in past stories, a wolf often was used to depict these very qualities in a person. In later versions of "Little Red Riding Hood," such as the version told by the Brothers Grimm, the wolf is killed by a conveniently nearby huntsman, but these versions generally have the same moral. Today, "Little Red Riding Hood" survives in many different forms, often involving werewolves of some sort, such as in the movie *Red Riding Hood* (2011),[229] and some renditions

---

[227] Perrault 13

[228] Perrault 13

[229] It is noteworthy that this film, unlike most werewolf films as well as other ridiculous retellings of "Little Red Riding Hood," is not actually terrible (even if the werewolf lore in the story is very Hollywoodian and stereotypically devilish). The film is quite good

of this tale go so far as to twist the narrative extensively, portraying Little Red Riding Hood as a werewolf or even as a monster hunter.

Two other fairytales that follow the example given in "Little Red Riding Hood" of a voracious wolf who meets his end due to his foolish gluttony are "The Wolf and the Fox" and "The Wolf and the Seven Young Kids." In "The Wolf and the Fox," the wolf is killed when he becomes overly greedy while attempting to steal food, and although the fox manages to escape the farmers chasing them both, the wolf is caught and killed because he ate too much meat and cannot run very fast. The titular wolf in "The Wolf and the Seven Young Kids" meets a fate similar to that of other wolves in later, more optimistic renditions of "Little Red Riding Hood," in that the wolf swallows whole six young goats and falls asleep; his belly is then cut open by the goat's mother, filled with rocks, and eventually he drowns in a river as a result of the weight in his stomach.

Much like other fairytales featuring wolves, Thomas

---

and, indeed, a prime example of enjoyable werewolf media despite what one may think of it as a romantic film.

Bewick's collection of Aesop's fables, which he published in 1818, features a wolf that is "innately evil, irreconcilably and fundamentally corrupt, and not very intelligent."[230] Although Aesop's wolf reflects the intelligence of the fox, the same aspects seen as positive in the fox are portrayed negatively in the wolf, deemed dishonesty instead of cleverness and cheating instead of craftiness. Likewise, wolves suffer a negative portrayal in the oral tradition of Isengrim the wolf and Reynard the fox: Isengrim is the villain, and he is often killed by the end of the story.[231] Generally speaking, the wolf in fairytales is a greedy, voracious, selfish, ungrateful, and generally malicious brute who is depicted as cunning at times and immensely unintelligent at others, and – more often than not – the wolf is defeated because of a combination of his gluttony (namely a tendency to swallow things whole) and his stupidity.

These examples and others are just a few of the many instances in which wolves are depicted as foolish, gluttonous,

---

[230] Lopez 255

[231] Lopez 259

and cruel villains in classical folk tales, but, unfortunately, other examples can also be found throughout most children's literature[232] and other works of fiction, notably including children's cartoons. A very recent example of this demonization appears in *My Little Pony: Friendship is Magic* (2010-), in which the pony Fluttershy, who can communicate with even the most seemingly vicious of animals, has a large group of woodland creatures who are her friends and companions. Her train of forest animals includes raccoons, ferrets, birds, beavers, rabbits, insects, spiders, badgers, and more, notably snakes and a bear. However, an ordinary wolf remains yet unseen in the series, as the only wolf-like creatures are the Timberwolves, malevolent monsters with whom even Fluttershy apparently cannot communicate, who attack the protagonists every time they appear and are easily dispatched, making the depiction of wolves in this series largely a negative

---

[232] One of the few exceptions is *The Jungle Book* by Rudyard Kipling, in which the wolves are a positive force, especially since they adopt Mowgli and serve as his immediate family. Many Western adaptations, most notably Disney's, often spurn the wolves' importance.

one. Later in the series, however, there is an ordinary, non-hyper-violent wolf glimpsed in one episode.

One of the very worst offenders who portray wolves as malevolent and overly hostile, however, is Walt Disney Studios, which historically has almost never portrayed wolves in a remotely decent light. The few benevolent wolf characters who have appeared in Disney Studios stories only ever do so very briefly, such as the wolves in *The Jungle Book* (1967), despite these wolves having a large role in the original *Jungle Book* stories by Rudyard Kipling. Indeed, Disney Studios seems to see wolves as the standard minor, throwaway villains for heroes to encounter randomly and fight in the wilderness, and they are always unbelievably aggressive, far more so than any real wolf – as are the wolves seen in countless video games[233] and other forms of media. Examples of such depictions of wolves by Disney Studios include the wolves in *Beauty and the Beast* (1991), *Frozen* (2013), and *The Sword in the Stone* (1963). Likewise, Disney Studios has other villainous wolves in other

---

[233] Wolves are among the most stereotypical of "low-level," easy creatures to massacre in assorted video games, especially role-playing games and anything with survival themes.

cartoons, such as the evil and inept Big Bad Wolf, as well as the Sheriff of Nottingham in *Robin Hood* (1973), a film that features many anthropomorphic animals, but only one major wolf character – who is, of course, villainous and incompetent, as are his wolf minions. Likewise, the wolves and werewolves in C. S. Lewis's *The Chronicles of Narnia* are wholly evil. Malevolent wolves are not, of course, confined solely to children's works, but appear in adult fiction as well. An example can be found in the film *The Grey* (2011), which is quite possibly the most ridiculous, inaccurate, and outright offensive portrayal of wolves to date – and that is quite a feat. It is films such as *The Grey* that further drive the concept of hyper-aggressive, dangerous wolves and thus lead to people fearing and even hating wolves. Much like malevolent werewolves in fiction, wolves and wolfish creatures are almost always irredeemable villains of some sort, and they are nearly always killed or otherwise defeated by a hero or heroes.

A creature related to wolves that crosses an interesting line between positive and negative portrayals in both real life and fiction is the wolfdog: any canine that is part wolf, part dog. Wolfdogs have long been ridiculed as pets and companions, and they are considered to be unpredictable and dangerous due to their wolf blood. However, wolfdogs generally receive a more positive reception in entertainment than do wolves themselves, even while real wolfdogs often suffer under harsh laws. For instance, the 1995 animated film *Balto* retells a fictional version of the true story about Balto the sled dog; however, the film changes Balto from a husky into a wolfdog-husky mix, and the character is mistreated and judged for his wolf blood. Ultimately, to deliver the medicine to the sick during an outbreak of illness, Balto must make peace with his wolf blood, and he howls alongside a white wolf as he embraces his inner strength and uses it to complete his mission; although wolves are misunderstood and misjudged by characters throughout the film, including Balto himself, many of them ultimately realize that it was Balto's wolf heritage that saved the day. Likewise, wolfdogs are portrayed positively in *White Fang*, a famous story by Jack London, in which the protagonist – White Fang, a wolfdog who is three-quarters wolf, one-quarter dog – comes from a wolf pack, is tamed, and saves the life of a human character before he settles down with a dog mate and becomes the companion to humans; in this story, wolves and wolfdogs alike are portrayed positively. Jack London also portrayed wolves in a positive light in his book *The Call of the Wild*, in which a St. Bernard-Scotch Shepherd dog named Buck runs off and joins a wolf pack. Thus, although negativity still surrounds them today, wolfdogs have occasionally been portrayed as sympathetic by entertainment, and Jack London's novels offer a refreshingly positive conception of wolves and their kin.

As seen in the previous chapter,[234] werewolves are often portrayed in an immensely negative light, as dangerous and violent monsters – but, today, there is arising a new association between werewolves and disease. It has become increasingly common for werewolves to be portrayed as almost nonthreatening, with their only danger being the "disease" they carry – instead of werewolves being depicted as powerful, rare monsters, they are portrayed as weak victims of an epidemic, thus crossing boundaries between werewolves and today's wildly popular concept of zombies, who themselves

---

[234] Chapter IV – The Moon Waxes: The Werewolf Popularity Surge

have retroactively adopted the act of spreading their nature by bite, as werewolves do. One such example of this werewolf-zombie cross-over can be found in the video game *World of Warcraft: Cataclysm*,[235] in which the worgen[236] are essentially compared to a plague of rats. Indeed, the worgen curse spreads so rapidly through Gilneas (the land in which the epidemic takes place) that there are worgen everywhere, literally overrunning the city, to the point that trying to move between buildings leaves the player wading through seas of worgen that fill the streets. The player must later massacre worgen in droves by blindly firing cannon shots into innumerable hordes of the beasts. *Cataclysm* provides just one example of how entertainment media today has begun to portray lycanthropy as an epidemic rather than as a unique and frightening curse

---

[235] An expansion pack to the popular MMORPG (Massively Multiplayer Online Role-Playing Game) *World of Warcraft*, as mentioned in Chapter IV of this study.

[236] The setting's term for werewolves. Many settings today prefer to call werewolves something other than simply "werewolves," or at the very least they are called "lycans" (a mutilation of the word "lycanthrope"), for whatever reason. Werewolves today are also occasionally referred to as "weres," although this term makes no etymological sense, as the word "were" simply means "man."

meaningfully bestowed upon an individual, which results in that individual turning into an almost unstoppable monster, who is so powerful that an entire movie can be spent attempting to defeat only one werewolf. Ironically, after zombie media took from werewolf media the idea of a curse or infection spreading by bite, now entertainment featuring werewolves has decided that werewolves themselves can be like the unimpressive zombies who are only a threat because they are mindless hostiles that carry some kind of disease and move in hordes. Not only does this portrayal continue the degradation of werewolf legends, but it also portrays real wolves in a negative light: as if wolves themselves are little more than a completely destructive plague that must be destroyed before they overpopulate, leading to acts such as wolf culling, even though wolf populations are not unusually high or, indeed, high at all.[237]

Negative portrayals of werewolves and wolves are

---

[237] Other stories also perpetuate this unfortunate and ridiculous trope, such as the video games *Bloodborne* with its werewolf-like enemies and *The Order: 1886*, neither of which are worth discussing more extensively than this footnote.

often attributed at least in part to the ancient societies who had to contend much more actively with wolves than people do today, and thus they feared and hated wolves for making their lives difficult by killing livestock[238]; yet some peoples, such as Native Americans, who struggled with the wolf chose instead to embrace it for its positive qualities. Among many tribes "[t]he wolf was also held in high regard because, though he was a fiercely loyal familial animal, he was also one who took the role of provider for the larger community (for carrion eaters like the fox and the raven). This was something that tribal Indians [Native Americans] understood very well, for in difficult times a man had the dual responsibility of feeding his own family as well as others."[239] Various Native American cultures remain among the most prominent societies to revere the wolf instead of shun it: "This association with, and imitation of, the wolf among American Indians was absolutely

---

[238] An extensive argument on its own, the idea of wolves versus livestock. Unfortunately, it would require a tangent from this study to detail why wolf cullings under the pretense of saving livestock are a bad idea.

[239] Lopez 104

pervasive,"[240] and they even believed "that to kill a wolf was to invite retribution from other wolves. ... And there was a widespread belief that a weapon that had killed a wolf would never work right again."[241] Unlike many Western civilizations, Native Americans saw the positive qualities of wolves in their blending of individualism with serving their society and protecting their families and packmates. These are the qualities that, today, society needs to recognize in wolves, instead of the baseless negative qualities with which wolves have become associated.[242]

Further respect for wolves from the Native Americans can be found in a story retold by Adam Douglas in his book *The*

---

[240] Lopez 105

[241] Lopez 109

[242] It is worth specifying that not *every* Native American tribe saw wolves in a positive light – only the overwhelming majority. Navajo, however, most notably have malevolent werewolf legends: "The Navajo word for wolf, *mai-coh*, is a synonym for witch. There is a good deal of witchcraft among the Navajo and belief in werewolves provides explanations for otherwise inexplicable (to them) phenomena. Witchcraft and werewolves are (the belief is current) more on the minds of some Navajos than others" (Lopez 123). Navajo werewolves killed others and "raided graveyards and mutilated bodies" (Lopez 123), not unlike some werewolf beliefs in Europe.

Beast Within: A History of the Werewolf. Douglas details a Native American totem legend, which he attributes to the Wolf clan, in northwestern Canada, in a place called Towq.[243] The totem of Towq is crowned with a wolf head, because, during a time when the town was starving, a shaman named Kamlugyides heard wolf howls and went to investigate. The shaman came upon a wolf and "called out to [it],"[244] prompting the wolf to approach.[245] The wolf had a bone stuck in its throat, and Kamlugyides removed it. Grateful, the wolf licked him before rejoining its pack. Days later, however, Kamlugyides heard the howling again, "but this time it seemed to be calling out for Kalmugyides."[246] He found the wolf once more, and, happily, it led him to the body of a deer, which the shaman used to feed his village. The wolf brought Kalmugyides a deer each day,

---

[243] Douglas 45-46

[244] Douglas 45

[245] This, of course, implies that either Kamlugyides can speak to animals, or else the wolf simply understood him. Given the wolf did not react violently, that aspect alone provides a more positive depiction of wolves than commonly seen, even in folklore. Animals, at times, have been shown to have a tendency to approach humans when they are in need of help, but the point still stands.

[246] Douglas 45

allowing his people to survive through their time of famine.

Today, due in no small part to the oppressively pervasive negativity imposed upon wolves and their mythological kin, wolves are often seen as dangerous pests that must be eliminated. In his book *Of Wolf and Man*, Barry Lopez deeply examines such beliefs, as he says, "I talked with men who saw nothing wrong with killing wolves, who felt it was basically a good thing to be doing."[247] For some individuals, Lopez determines that this hatred, which "they [struggled] to put it into words,"[248] comes from a feeling that "wolves seemed better off than they [the hunters] were."[249] Although "We forget how little, really, separates us from the times and circumstances in which we, too, would have killed wolves,"[250] there nonetheless exists today a struggle against those who would kill wolves for reasons not properly justified by science or anything else. In ages past, and to some extent event today, wolves have been the victims of baseless destruction and even

---

[247] Lopez 137

[248] Lopez 138

[249] Lopez 138

[250] Lopez 138

torture, including individuals who "set wolves on fire and tore their jaws out and cut their Achilles tendons and turned dogs loose on them. They poisoned them with strychnine, arsenic, and cyanide, on such a scale that *millions* of other animals ... were killed incidentally in the process. In the thick of the wolf fever they even poisoned themselves, and burned down their own property torching the woods to get rid of wolf havens."[251] In the mid-1800s in the United States, wolves were slaughtered with extreme dedication, and today they are chased using airplanes, helicopters, and snowmobiles until they collapse from exhaustion. They are killed for entertainment rather than even attempting an excuse, and "[i]n Minnesota in the 1970s people choked Eastern timber wolves to death in snares to show their contempt for the animal's designation as an endangered species."[252]

No matter the arguments claiming that such extreme hunting of wolves is not actually so cruel and unreasonable as it seems, wolves have long been regarded by society with hatred

---

[251] Lopez 139

[252] Lopez 139

and fear that is displayed toward no other species of animal. Lopez provides countless more examples of the slaughter and torture of wolves throughout his book, which are far too numerous and extensive to retell here, leading to the simple question: why do humans harbor such great hatred and fear of the wolf? As Lopez mentions, this hatred and fear exist in part due to "theriophobia. Fear of the beast. Fear of the beast as an irrational, violent, insatiable creature. Fear of the projected beast in oneself. ... [T]heriophobia is projected onto a single animal, the animal becomes a scapegoat, and it is annihilated. That is what happened to the wolf in America."[253] The answer to the question as to why and how the wolf came to be the target of such hatred lies, quite simply, in the explorations behind werewolf and wolf beliefs already detailed throughout this study. As stated by Lopez,

> The hatred has religious roots: the wolf was the Devil in disguise. And it has secular roots: wolves killed stock and made men poor. At a more general level it had to

---

[253] Lopez 140. Indeed, it also happened to wolves across many regions of the world, including England and Ireland.

do, historically, with feelings about wilderness. What men said about the one, they generally meant about the other. To celebrate wilderness was to celebrate the wolf; to want an end to wilderness and all it stood for was to want the wolf's head.[254]

When mankind began to build great civilizations, the wolf got in the way. Lopez equates wolves to an embodiment of wilderness, and "the act of killing wolves became a symbolic act, a way to lash out at that enormous, inchoate obstacle: wilderness."[255]

Such hatred and fear of the wolf began in Europe and spread to the rest of the world, with the greatest basis for this fear of wolves being that they were seen as wild animals, as killers of livestock, as predators with a frightening appearance – and as creatures that reflect many of mankind's own social and behavioral qualities, but in a primal and untamed manner that disturbed the minds of most people. After all, was it not from a relative of wolves that humans acquired the

---

[254] Lopez 140
[255] Lopez 141

domesticated dogs now called "man's best friend"? Wolves and humans have an undeniable association and connection, and from these fears of seeing one's reflection in the terrifying wolf arose the werewolf: the combination of man and an animal (one that almost mirrors many of man's qualities and social behaviors) that many civilizations feared. Conversely, from the *positive* aspects of wolves rose the benevolent werewolf, associated with the desirable traits of the wolf as opposed to the negative ones. One could spend a great deal of time detailing the wide variety of negative writings about wolves themselves, not in a fictional sense or through fictional portrayals, but real ones – even Theodore Roosevelt called the wolf he so hated "'the beast of waste and desolation.'"[256]

A hatred for wolves is ingrained in humans from a young age by the endless children's stories of evil wolves, and then exacerbated by media portraying violent and malevolent werewolves, and the time has come for these portrayals to change. Society today enjoys touting its superiority to the "medieval" mind and "medieval" ideas, which are often

---

[256] Lopez 142

considered primitive and even silly, yet contemporary society has done nothing but embrace the negative image of the wolf: "The medieval mind, more than any other mind in history, was obsessed with the image of wolves. ... Anything that threatened a peasant's precarious existence was 'the wolf.'"[257] As Lopez also states, "The wolf ... continues to generate more adamant positions and to trigger more powerful emotions than any other large predator ... Some folklore about wolves ... is so deeply entrenched that its adherents completely shut out the emerging insights of field biologists, historians, religion scholars, and other researchers in the social sciences and humanities. In their rigid stances they are impervious even to reason."[258] Mankind's positive relationship with the wolf has, so far, lasted only long enough for man to domesticate the dog in ancient times. The dog, man still reveres, but the wolf, his wild ancestor – without whom the dog could not exist – man now wishes only to slaughter.

Undoubtedly, the increasingly negative portrayals of

---

[257] Lopez 206

[258] Lopez 292

werewolves throughout history have exerted terrible influence upon man's destructive view of real wolves, and in addition, such portrayals disrespect and dismiss the considerable annals of legends – all far deeper and more moral than the simplistic werewolf stories of today – that created the werewolf myth. In ages past, werewolves were used in various ways, such as devices to question mankind's humanity,[259] to tell tales of individuals so noble and chivalrous that they retain their goodness despite their transformation,[260] to highlight the positive aspects of the animal and encourage man to reflect those aspects,[261] and finally, to test a man's true nature.[262]

---

[259] This concept is, arguably, the basis for almost any werewolf tale: what makes someone human? Can someone still be human, if they take the guise of an animal?

[260] Namely the assorted medieval stories, such as *Bisclavret*, which have a noble werewolf (often a knight) who retains his manners even when in werewolf form. Such tales were covered in Chapter II of this study.

[261] As seen in many Norse stories, as covered in Chapter II of this study.

[262] The werewolf curse was bestowed upon individuals to test their humanity in various stories, including some Christian stories (as discussed in Chapter II of this study), as well as ancient tales, such as the rituals of Arcadia (as covered in Chapter I of this study).

Today, as extensively covered in Chapter IV of this study, the variously helpful, protective, benevolent, chivalrous, noble werewolves are gone, as are those who serve to highlight interesting moral questions, offer an examination into the connection between man and beast, and explore what it is exactly to "be human." Werewolves need not be limited to simple plot devices, e.g. mindless monsters, that only create a conflict, a jump scare in a film, or a random enemy encounter in a video game. Ignorance has led to the dismissal of werewolves as nothing more than the simplistic, contrived, often teased, and standardized monster into which Hollywood turned them for the purpose of creating horror films or to get a laugh from the audience, rather than the fascinating conception deeply ingrained in the minds of humans, such that belief in werewolves has existed since before the dawn of recorded history. Not only is such ignorance a slight upon the innumerable, mystifying legends that appear in almost every culture around the world, but such simple negativity serves only to reinforce mankind's age-old baseless fear and hatred of wolves themselves.

Many werewolf stories throughout history have proven

that, originally, werewolves were seen as representing aspects far more important than the trivial monsters to which they have been degraded today – both tales that were believed to be true, and tales that were not (such as *Bisclavret*). Werewolves today are not only created in ignorance, with a total lack of knowledge about the legends and certainly lacking in any respect for their historical and moral value, but also so simplistic that they have become nothing more than the jump-scare monster in a B-list film, a meaningless zombie plague, an unremarkable monster randomly encountered in a video game, or the "monster of the week" in a TV show. All of these portrayals have resulted in the word "werewolf" often degrading the value of a story to the point that many will dismiss it as "cheesy" and lose interest the moment they realize werewolves are involved, particularly as these stereotypical werewolf portrayals today have become increasingly predictable, exhausted, and above all, utterly meaningless. Returning werewolves to their legendary roots could dramatically improve the richness of the stories themselves, and could also create more interest in the myths of many cultures worldwide throughout history, as well as raise interesting questions about morality, the nature of man and animal and their relationships, an exploration of civilization and wilderness, and what it means to be human. More importantly, this renewal could be taken a step farther: the occasional portrayal of the outright *benevolent* werewolf – as opposed to the relentlessly negative, malicious portrayals of werewolves today – could improve not only the aforementioned aspects of the story and provide for a more interesting and thematic narrative, but it could also serve to begin the slow process of reversing society's deeply ingrained, negative view of wolves themselves.

As an aspiring author, I am using my own fiction to explore different portrayals of werewolves, especially benevolent ones, in an attempt to pursue some of these ideas. My first self-published novel, *Wulfgard: The Prophecy of the Six, Book I – Knightfall,* is an ancient-medieval dark fantasy story that centers on Sir Tom Drake, a knight who discovers that he has a mysterious connection to werewolves (ancient and feared shapeshifters resulting from a curse most often spread by bite; they are extremely dangerous, almost impossible to kill, and thought to be nothing more than malevolent monsters) after a white werewolf stalks him in a forest. The entirety of *The Prophecy of the Six* series focuses on werewolves in this setting, called Wulfgard, in which my brother and I plan to publish many more stories. Indeed, werewolves are a centerpiece of the entire setting itself, and the core of the story involves exploring the protagonist, lycanthropy, and the various aforementioned themes, morals, and ideas regarding werewolves. In this series and other stories I plan to write, I hope personally to create more meaningful werewolf characters, and werewolf lore in itself, to prove that werewolves need not be so simplistic and malevolent.

Benevolent werewolves in entertainment media have the potential to become a very important first step in many directions: fostering more interest in, and respect for, the ancient legends of many cultures around the world (some of which are still believed today), as opposed to treating these stories with nothing more than lack of interest or outright ignorance of their very existence; creating deeper and more interesting werewolf stories and characters in general, thus removing werewolves from their association with low-quality entertainment; raising interesting moral and existential questions; and, of course, providing portrayals of wolves and wolf-related creatures that are not destructive. Teaching society about real wolves through science and research is effective, but only in so far as it reaches those who truly need to hear it – however, entertainment is a far more all-encompassing field, and the stories told through books, movies, TV shows, video games, and more, affect people in deep and profound ways on a subconscious level, of which even the audiences themselves may not be aware. If positive portrayals of werewolves and wolves alike appeared more often (or, indeed, at all) in entertainment, thus lessening the negativity toward them through benevolent and desirable portrayals, they could become the first major steps to undoing humankind's thousands of years misrepresenting, mistreating, and misunderstanding not only werewolf legends, but wolves themselves. They could yet turn around the overwhelming ignorance of the culturally rich werewolf legends from ages past and dismissal of werewolves in fiction due to their lack of complexity and their focus on ironic comedy to drive home the idea that werewolves cannot and never should be taken seriously, as well as the eons of extreme hatred and fear for animals that are no more evil beings of destruction, insanity, and bloodlust than are their descendants: mankind's precious and loyal canine pets so increasingly revered in society today.

MAEGAN A. STEBBINS

Conclusion – Turning the Tables

Negative portrayals of werewolves and wolves continue to thrive, resulting in both ignorance of virtually countless werewolf legends that were once believed throughout the world, as well as misconceptions and stigmas forced upon wolves that exist even today. Despite the beliefs of many ancient cultures regarding neutral or benevolent werewolves, and despite the reverence with which wolves themselves were once treated by our ancestors across the world, society today has chosen to condemn the wolf to being seen as a creature of evil and destruction. Entertainment has a far more powerful influence upon an individual's beliefs than many people would like to acknowledge, on both conscious and subconscious levels, and this effect is especially seen in developing children, whose conceptions are easily formed by the stories they are told as they grow. However, children's stories are perhaps the greatest offenders when it comes to negative portrayals of wolves (and, increasingly, werewolves, with many children's novels featuring them as villains as well), and as children grow older, they find even more media in which wolves – and their counterpart, werewolves – are depicted as malevolent.

These over-abundant malevolent portrayals of werewolves and wolves directly influence society's view of the real wolves that live around the globe – or, at least, the wolves that have managed to survive the coordinated extinction efforts put forth by humans. If cultures were to abandon the stereotype that wolves – and, in the case of fantasy, their cursed, half-human counterparts – are evil by including more positive portrayals of wolves and werewolves in entertainment media, this change could be the first step in reversing the eons of unfounded hatred and fear with which humanity has regarded the wolf for far too long. Wolves exist with humans as do other living creatures – they are related to our domesticated dogs, and, like dogs, they have their own instincts and feelings, none of which are inherently "evil" or "unintelligent," as entertainment so often portrays. Wolves have received an unbearable amount of cruelty from humans throughout history, and their suffering has not lessened in modern times – indeed, perhaps it has increased, with the use of many modern and exceptionally inhumane traps and hunting methods. Although positive portrayals of wolves in entertainment may not immediately affect the treatment of wolves today (an issue that desperately needs to be addressed), changing the image of the wolf, the werewolf, the wolfdog, and other wolfish creatures could be the first major step toward a world in which humans show toward wolves understanding, respect, and sympathy.

Wolves represent a mirror through which humanity perceives themselves: we share much in common with wolves, including but not limited to strong social bonds and needs, an incredibly wide range of emotions and displays of genuine affection, respect and mourning for the dead, the importance of family, putting others before oneself, taking care of the injured and infirm, the intelligence to work in groups, and even, in a manner of speaking, a love for singing and expressing oneself, both alone and with others. These among many other factors makes the connection between wolves and humans a natural one that results in werewolves having appeared in legends throughout every culture that lives in proximity to wolves and throughout the entirety of unrecorded and recorded history. Werewolves are, indeed, a look into ourselves: they are the ultimate form of life that prehistoric humans, and humans for so many eras afterward, sought to embody and achieve in order to survive and thrive in the wilderness while maintaining their nobility and society. What does it say about us, then, that we now portray werewolves as evil? What does it say about us, then, that humanity as a whole seeks so greedily to destroy wolves and cease sharing the world with them?

As explored throughout this study, werewolves of legend were not the simplistically malevolent, often outright stupid, and frequently comical, standardized monsters with contrived weaknesses and bloodlust, or else simply humanoid domesticated dogs, as popular culture portrays them today. In the past, werewolves were often developed in legend and in fiction to highlight a moral in a story, to blur and to bring into question the connections between human and beast, and to convey the primality that still exists in every person – for better or for worse. Werewolves were not always seen as negative entities of evil, instead being neutral or, sometimes, even benevolent: as protectors, and as shamans, healers, powerful warriors, and noble knights. The idea of lycanthropy had layers of interesting meanings that could be investigated in far more depth, such as the previously mentioned barrier between man and animal – and primality and civilization – that werewolves so boldly cross. As fictional creatures, werewolves are capable of bringing far more to a story than they currently do to entertainment, as is highlighted by the numerous legends that popular culture has carelessly overlooked and all but designated to be forgotten, leading to widespread ignorance of the worldwide werewolf myth and the now virtually inescapable association of werewolves with sub-par media and even comedy. The return of the benevolent werewolf in fiction carries the potential to not only bring morality, complexity, and thought-provoking themes back to stories focusing on werewolves (which are, right now, still derided as drivel, and generally rightfully so), but also to bring attention to many fascinating legends in folklore throughout the entire world – many of which serve not only to tell us more about various cultures, but also serve to highlight the morals of said cultures, which are now all but forgotten, while also aiding in the slow

171

process of reversing society's negative view of wolves.

For lycanthropy, there remains much to be remembered, to be said, and to be explored – for, after all, the ancient legend of the werewolf would not continue to haunt and captivate us since prehistory and into our culture today if humanity did not still hold that same, undying fascination turned fear: that a wolf lives within us all.

MAEGAN A. STEBBINS

Bibliography & Reviews

For the sake of clarity, I am going to provide very brief reviews for each of my bibliographic sources. I could review many sources far too extensively to be condensed here, but in the interest of maintaining focus, I shall attempt to keep each review relatively short and mostly regarding the source's usefulness, accuracy, general quality, and – when it comes to entertainment – storytelling value and quality of the werewolves portrayed therein.

Due to my highly impassioned nature, for better or for worse, these reviews may contain sarcasm and strong opinions that are not otherwise considered professional.

Primary Sources

Altered Beast [Video game]. (1988). Sega.

> A fun game and certainly worth a play. Some modern video game players may find it difficult, however.

An American Werewolf in London. Dir. John Landis. Perf. David

173

Naughton and Jenny Agutter. Universal Pictures, 1981.
DVD.

Although a critically acclaimed werewolf movie, I
cannot say it's one of my favorites; it adds an
exceedingly strange element (that I do not care
for) to its werewolf lore in that the werewolf is
haunted by his victims and they attempt to drive
him to suicide. Indeed, it is also one of the
primary culprits in preventing modern audiences
from taking werewolves seriously, as it is
subversive and comedic in its own dark ways. But
the movie is an important part of modern
werewolf history and a must-watch for anyone
studying in the field, if not only for its
groundbreaking non-CGI transformation scene.
Beware the predictable ending. I personally blame
this film a great deal for taking steps toward
werewolves becoming comical, darkly ironic or
not, and I detest it for the legacy of self-aware
werewolf films that cannot let go of the concept

that characters in the story must all chuckle at the very idea of werewolves.

Baldur's Gate II: Shadows of Amn [Video game]. (2000). Wizards of the Coast.

Easily one of the greatest video games ever created and one of the best stories ever told, it is a masterpiece on every front. Although its gameplay is deeply enjoyable on a level achieved by precious few other games and the 2D artwork holds unique beauty, it is also worth playing for its unforgettable story alone. A full and in-depth review would be far too long to include here. The werewolves have a great design, to boot. Modern players are encouraged to overlook what they may so falsely perceive as an "outdated" game and experience the masterpiece. Modern players are also implored to overlook the "Enhanced Editions" of the Baldur's Gate games in favor of playing the unmodified originals, as it is far from the same game experience.

Baldur's Gate II: Throne of Bhaal [Video game]. (2001). Wizards of the Coast.

> See *Baldur's Gate 2: Shadows of Amn*. Although some consider this game to be linear compared to its predecessors, its relative linearity is necessary in order to properly conclude the epic saga.

Balto. Dir. Simon Wells. Perf. Kevin Bacon and Bridget Fonda. Amblimation, 1995. DVD.

> One of my favorite animated movies, with exceptionally beautiful art and music (the sequence of Balto and the white wolf in the snow is easily one of my favorite moments in any film), in spite of inaccuracies to the true story of Balto. I very highly recommend watching it.

Barber, Richard, trans. *Bestiary*. 1300s. Rochester, NY: Boydell, 1999. Print.

> A good bestiary, with original medieval illuminations included. Recommended for anyone interested in medieval history and folklore.

Baring-Gould, Sabine. "Jean Grenier, a French Werewolf."

1603. *A Lycanthropy Reader: Werewolves in Western Culture.*
Ed. Charlotte F. Otten. Syracuse, NY: Syracuse UP, 1986.
62-69. Print.

> Although an obviously extrapolated retelling of
> Jean Grenier's confessions in court that is too
> exaggerated and assuming at times, namely with
> small details, Baring-Gould nonetheless writes
> well. Most werewolf scholars are familiar with
> Grenier; a recommended read, if not only for a
> glimpse into how incredibly the perception of
> werewolves changed over time into beings like
> Grenier.

Bayfield, Robert. "A Treatise." 1663. *A Lycanthropy Reader:*
Werewolves in Western Culture. Ed. Charlotte F. Otten.
Syracuse, NY: Syracuse UP, 1986. 47-49. Print.

> An extremely short account of a case of, as he calls
> it, wolf madness, Bayfield's treatise is most useful
> simply to emphasize the fact that many doctors
> and scholars of his era echoed each other
> regarding the symptoms of what they thought
> drove people to believe in werewolves in their

THE WEREWOLF: PAST AND FUTURE

desperate search for a scientific "explanation" as
to the belief in them.

Beauty and the Beast. Dir. Gary Trousdale and Kirk Wise. Perf.
Paige O'Hara and Robby Benson. Walt Disney
Productions, 1991. DVD.

> Unarguably a masterpiece both as an animated
> film and as a film in general, despite its
> stereotypical portrayal of preposterously
> aggressive wolves. There is little else to say. Its
> assorted counterparts and potential remakes
> could never compare.

Boguet, Henri. "Of the Metamorphosis of Men into Beasts."
1590. *A Lycanthropy Reader: Werewolves in Western Culture.*
Ed. Charlotte F. Otten. Syracuse, NY: Syracuse UP, 1986.
77-91. Print.

> An extensive look into werewolves, but dated and
> biased. Boguet is nonetheless a good source for
> opinions from the time (particularly as he displays
> the late medieval transition into the Early Modern
> period when it comes to werewolf beliefs), while

also providing an interesting overview of several beliefs about lycanthropy. Highly recommended for those in the field.

Burton, Robert. "Diseases of the Mind." 1621. *A Lycanthropy Reader: Werewolves in Western Culture*. Ed. Charlotte F. Otten. Syracuse, NY: Syracuse UP, 1986. 45-47. Print.

Essentially, the longer and more robust piece that Bayfield seemed to draw from for his own short treatise. Burton's piece, though fairly short, is a very useful and important part of werewolf lore of the 1600s.

Cambrensis, Giraldus. "A Wolf Which Conversed with a Priest." 1187. *A Lycanthropy Reader: Werewolves in Western Culture*. Ed. Charlotte F. Otten. Syracuse, NY: Syracuse UP, 1986. 57-62. Print.

This is perhaps one of the best little werewolf tales ever told, and it was told as a true story, rather than fiction. It is simple and highlights that Christianity has not always portrayed wolves and werewolves as evil, and indeed, to judge a wolf by its being a wolf is to judge someone by their exterior and is wrong.

Cooper, John. "Monster." *Awake*. Skillet. Lava Records, 2009. CD.

> One of my favorite songs, by a favorite band.

Dark Shadows. ABC. New York, NY, 1966-1971. Television.

> An essential part of monster pop culture history, this show lasted for many years and told some interesting, if increasingly convoluted, stories. Recommended, if you can dedicate enough time to watching it.

Deacon, John, and John Walker. "Spirits and Devils." 1601. *A Lycanthropy Reader: Werewolves in Western Culture*. Ed. Charlotte F. Otten. Syracuse, NY: Syracuse UP, 1986. 129-135. Print.

> A piece that is even more ridiculous than usual when it comes to old writings on lycanthropy. Interesting, but overall, it is still little more than yet another condemnation of lycanthropy and believers in it, this one even more extreme than usual (and offering little to no additional

information otherwise). Could potentially be useful, but not a highly necessary reading for those studying folklore.

de France, Marie. "The Lay of the Were-Wolf." 1170. *A Lycanthropy Reader: Werewolves in Western Culture.* Ed. Charlotte F. Otten. Syracuse, NY: Syracuse UP, 1986. 256-262. Print.

Bisclavret is very likely my single favorite werewolf story ever told, and Marie de France's lays are all very enjoyable. Anyone studying werewolves, broader folklore, or even general literature or history should be familiar with this story.

Diablo II [Video game]. (2000). Blizzard Entertainment.

Almost certainly the best game in the *Diablo* series due to my personal biases. A fun game, especially with friends, and undeniably a classic. I like the werewolf design.

Dog Soldiers. Dir. Neil Marshall. Perf. Sean Pertwee and Kevin McKidd. Pathé, 2002. DVD.

I do not care for this film, and I have little more to say otherwise. It is a celebration of everything wrong with most modern werewolf portrayals (though it is not new enough to contain some of the even more unfortunate, newer tropes). I realize it is popular; I simply disagree. Not recommended whatsoever.

Draiman, David. "The Animal." *Asylum*. Disturbed. Reprise Records, 2010. CD.

A song that embodies the general idea of the evil, Satanic werewolf, especially if you watch the accompanying music video. An excellent song by a good band, regardless.

The Elder Scrolls III: Bloodmoon [Video game]. (2003). Bethesda Softworks.

Easily the best portrayal of werewolves ever featured in a video game, and Bethesda's best game even without expansions. I still revisit this classic simply to enjoy the virtually flawless playable werewolf experience again. The werewolf design is excellent. Very highly recommend it.

The Elder Scrolls V: Skyrim [Video game]. (2011). Bethesda

Softworks.

> A critically acclaimed but rather lifeless game, even though it can fun it can be for a few hours, or so I hear. Mods do not extend the game's lifespan for me, personally. The werewolf quests are worth a run. The werewolf mechanics are quite fun and alone make the game worth playing for a little while, although I recommend playing *The Elder Scrolls III: Morrowind* and its expansions instead, particularly *Bloodmoon*. Regardless, Skyrim is still a decent game, I suppose, particularly if you are hungry to play as a powerful werewolf, but it does not have any of the mechanics to make you feel like a victim of lycanthropy as opposed to someone who possesses a controllable superpower, unlike *Bloodmoon*. As a brief aside, avoid *Elder Scrolls Online* if you enjoy the setting's werewolf lore, as ESO's handling of werewolves outright spurns and insults all previous installments.

Endore, Guy. *The Werewolf of Paris*. New York, NY: Pegasus

Crime, 2013. Print.

> Far from one of my favorite werewolf stories,
> particularly since the werewolf has more in
> common with a vampire, and not an enjoyable
> read either way. I do not recommend it.

Ford, John. *The Lover's Melancholy. The Dramatic Works of
Massinger and Ford.* Comp. Hartley Coleridge. London:
Routledge, Warne, and Routledge, 1840. 532-553. *Internet
Archive.* Web.
<https://archive.org/details/dramaticworksma04colegoog
>.

> A strange play and a strange portrayal of
> werewolves, as well, but typical of its time period.
> Take it or leave it; not a necessary read, though it
> is good to be informed on the werewolf
> appearances in plays of this period.

Frankenstein Meets the Wolf Man. Dir. Roy William Neill. Perf.
Lon Chaney, Jr. and Ilona Massey. Universal Pictures,
1943. DVD.

> An unconventional story, but a fun watch. Not as

necessary to werewolf lore as *The Wolf Man* itself,

though still highly influential. Recommended.

Frozen. Dir. Chris Buck and Jennifer Lee. Perf. Kristen Bell and

Idina Menzel. Walt Disney Productions, 2013. DVD.

> It would be a bit ridiculous not to recommend this
> instant classic. Ignore the stereotypically
> bloodthirsty, absurdly aggressive, and
> unintelligent, blue-eyed wolves (feral huskies?),
> because it is an excellent film. Also be sure to
> watch *Tangled* because I would be remiss not to
> mention it as one of my favorite Disney films or
> films in general; just saying.

Gaiman, Neil. *The Graveyard Book*. New York, NY:

HarperCollins, 2008. Print.

> A fun book to read, although it is simply a much
> lesser revision of Rudyard Kipling's *The Jungle
> Books*, so I recommend reading those first and/or
> instead. Still, Gaiman presents a reasonably
> interesting setting and certainly breaks
> stereotypes with his werewolves, even if the story
> is predictable for anyone other than, perhaps, its

target youthful audience, and the werewolf

likewise meets a painfully predictable end.

Gontier, Adam. "Animal I Have Become." *One-X*. Three Days

Grace. Sony BMG, 2006. CD.

Another personal favorite song of mine, both as a

song and as a "werewolf song," although no

specific mention of werewolves is made.

Goulart, I. "Admirable Histories." 1607. *A Lycanthropy Reader:

Werewolves in Western Culture*. Ed. Charlotte F. Otten.

Syracuse, NY: Syracuse UP, 1986. 41-45. Print.

An interesting account of werewolf beliefs given

by a source considered very prestigious

historically. Highly recommended.

Gruenwald, Mark. *Captain America: Man & Wolf*. 1992. New

York, NY: Marvel, 2011. Print.

Easily my favorite comic and/or graphic novel, I

cannot recommend this enough as a superhero

fan, as a Captain America fan, or even as a

werewolf scholar. It is a genuine shame that these

issues receive such contempt from some comic

fans. Handles the werewolf storyline with
seriousness and intelligence, and the werewolves
accurately convey their emotions using their ears
and body posture. The opposite of all this praise
can be said about later rehashes of the Capwolf
story with different universes and/or characters.

Hetfield, James. "Of Wolf and Man." *Metallica*. Metallica.
Elektra Records, 1991. CD.

The only werewolf song featured in this study that
is positive in nature, and it is a good song
otherwise. I recommend it.

Housman, Clemence. *The Were-Wolf*. 1896. *A Lycanthropy
Reader: Werewolves in Western Culture*. Ed. Charlotte F.
Otten. Syracuse, NY: Syracuse UP, 1986. 286-321. Print.

I do not care for this allegory. It is a shame that so
many werewolf scholars feel the need to cite and
praise it. Little more than yet another
stereotypically evil werewolf portrayal. Despite
what some scholars claim, we cannot pin said
portrayal solely on Christianity, as Christianity is
responsible for several positive wolves and

werewolves.

The Howling. Dir. Joe Dante. Perf. Dee Wallace and Patrick
Macnee. AVCO Embassy Pictures, 1981. DVD.

> An incredibly negative film when it comes to
> werewolf portrayals and unfortunately a highly
> influential one. I particularly dislike the
> werewolves' association with sex. Overall, not
> something I care for, nor would I recommend it
> beyond the experience of seeing what is
> considered a classic werewolf movie. Frankly, I
> detest this film from the bottom of my heart and
> wish it had never been created.

James I. "Men-Woolfes." 1597. *A Lycanthropy Reader: Werewolves
in Western Culture.* Ed. Charlotte F. Otten. Syracuse, NY:
Syracuse UP, 1986. 127-129. Print.

> A short and simple piece, but highly
> recommended reading, if not only because it was
> written by King James I and thus highlights the
> power a belief in werewolves held during this time
> period.

The Jungle Book. Dir. Wolfgang Reitherman. Perf. Phil Harris

and Sebastian Cabot. Walt Disney Productions, 1967.

DVD.

> A fun movie, to be sure, and very enjoyable, if
> incredibly inaccurate to the source material to the
> point of downright disrespect, particularly where
> Kaa is concerned (the writers Westernize Kaa's
> role and nature in the story, making him a
> typically evil and unintelligent snake instead of an
> important mentor and friend to Mowgli). This in
> addition to the wolves being utterly snubbed
> results in a film that can be immensely frustrating
> for any fan of the original stories.

Kipling, Rudyard. *The Jungle Books*. 1894. New York, NY:

Bantam Dell, 2000. Print.

> An excellent and classic set of tales, although I do
> not at all care for the depressing ending.
> Regardless, fun stories and outstanding poems,
> particularly "The Law of the Jungle."

London, Jack. *Call of the Wild*. 1903. *Works of Jack London*. Ed.

Paul J. Horowitz. New York, NY: Crown, 1980. 15-74. Print.

An excellent novel; highly recommended.

---. *White Fang.* 1906. *Works of Jack London.* Ed. Paul J. Horowitz. New York, NY: Crown, 1980. 75-206. Print.

> Another classic by Jack London; also highly recommended.

Meyer, Stephenie. *New Moon.* New York, NY: Hachette Book Group, 2006. Print.

> This series receives much unnecessary hate, in which I thoughtlessly participated when the books first released. Upon giving them a chance, I found them decently enjoyable, although not really suited to my personal tastes. Regardless, they do not deserve the preposterous levels of stigma and hatred that they often receive, and indeed, Meyer actually did quite a bit of folkloric research and it shows in her books; she simply chose to diverge from it in her own ways. Not a favorite series of mine, but I do respect it and did enjoy it when I finally gave it the fair chance it deserves.

---. *Breaking Dawn.* New York, NY: Hachette Book Group, 2008.

Print.

> See *New Moon*. However, I remain annoyed that
> Meyer thought it best to retcon her initial concept
> of werewolves and turn the "good" werewolves
> into "shapeshifters" whereas the "real"
> werewolves, called werewolves, are stereotypical
> evil stupid killer monsters that were hunted
> basically to extinction.

My Little Pony: Friendship Is Magic. Hasbro. 2010-. Television.

> I truly enjoyed this show, although I do take issue
> with what was mentioned in this study.
> Regardless, it is an excellent cartoon, with many
> good stories and messages and fun jokes, as well
> as great music, even if it has gone down
> somewhat over time.

Ovid. *Metamorphoses*. 8. Trans. A. D. Melville. New York, NY:
Oxford UP, 2008. Print.

> A classic and a must-read for anyone studying
> most any kind of mythology and folklore.

Perrault, Charles. "Little Red Riding Hood." 1697. *The Classic
Fairy Tales*. Ed. Maria Tartar. New York, NY: Norton, 1999.

11-13. Print.

> The original as well as my personal favorite version of the classic fairytale – the one without the contrived happy ending featuring the woodsman.

Petronius. "Niceros's Story." 1st century A.D. *A Lycanthropy Reader: Werewolves in Western Culture*. Ed. Charlotte F. Otten. Syracuse, NY: Syracuse UP, 1986. 231-234. Print.

> An absolute must-read for anyone in the field.

Reynolds, George W. M. *Wagner the Wehr-wolf*. 1847. New York, NY: Hurst, 2016. Print.

> A predictable story, at least to a modern reader well-versed in typical werewolf lore of the more recent eras – in other words, the werewolf is created by a pact with the devil. Good to know about, not necessarily a good read.

Robin Hood. Dir. Wolfgang Reitherman. Perf. Phil Harris and Andy Devine. Walt Disney Productions, 1973. DVD.

> An excellent movie that I know by heart, and no doubt a classic, though I have always – even when

I was a child – taken qualm with the only wolf featured therein being an inept villain (even if he is one of the most amusing characters).

Rowling, J. K. *Harry Potter and the Prisoner of Azkaban.* New York, NY: Scholastic, 1999. Print.

An excellent book, and one of my personal favorites in the *Harry Potter* series. Read this book instead of watching its horrible film adaptation, which is by far the worst of the *Harry Potter* films (and not only because of the groundbreakingly atrocious werewolf design).

---. *Harry Potter and the Half-Blood Prince.* New York, NY: Scholastic, 2005. Print.

One of my personal favorite *Harry Potter* books after the series took a darker turn following the end of *Harry Potter and the Goblet of Fire.* A good read, and arguably better than the fifth *Harry Potter* book, but not nearly as enjoyable as earlier installments in the series.

Scot, Reginald. "Of Transformations." 1584. *A Lycanthropy Reader: Werewolves in Western Culture.* Ed. Charlotte F.

Otten. Syracuse, NY: Syracuse UP, 1986. 115-127. Print.

>A somewhat lengthy study on human transformation in various stories and cultures. Useful information. Recommended.

Stebbins, Maegan. *Wulfgard, The Prophecy of the Six – Book I: Knightfall*. Justin & Maegan Stebbins, 2015. Print.

>This is, obviously, my own novel, and it would be inappropriate for me to comment upon it. I will say, however, that *The Prophecy of the Six* series is the story I most want to tell. If I can accomplish nothing else in my life, I hope to at least put this series into existence, as this is, of all the fiction I plan to write, the story means everything to me. Revision to be published mid-2020s.

Stevenson, Robert Louis. *The Strange Case of Dr. Jekyll and Mr. Hyde*. 1886. New York, NY: Signet Classic, 2003. Print.

>An absolute classic, and one of the best human transformation stories ever told. Very highly recommend.

"Stubbe Peeter." 1590. *A Lycanthropy Reader: Werewolves in*

Western Culture. Ed. Charlotte F. Otten. Syracuse, NY: Syracuse UP, 1986. 69-77. Print.

> Undeniably a necessary read to anyone in the field, the account of Peter Stubbe highlights the fact that werewolf scholars hold a great deal of blame in distorting the modern-day image of the werewolf, despite the fact that Stubbe was clearly a sorcerer during his own time period.

Summers, Montague, trans. *The Malleus Maleficarum.* 1486. Lexington, KY: n.p., 2015. Print.

> Montague Summers provides an excellent translation of the *Malleus Maleficarum*, which should be on the shelf of anyone studying legends of the occult.

The Sword in the Stone. Dir. Wolfgang Reitherman. Perf. Rickie Sorensen and Karl Swenson. Walt Disney Productions, 1963. DVD.

> One of my favorite Disney films and animated films in general, despite its predictable portrayal of wolves, same as virtually all other Disney creations. An excellent and funny classic, and a

must-see for any fan of all things medieval.

Teen Wolf. Dir. Rod Daniel. Perf. Michael J. Fox and Susan

Ursitti. Atlantic Releasing Corporation, 1985. DVD.

> A good movie, though it can feel a little boring, as
> it largely serves as a showcase of music at times. I
> should dislike it intensely, given it arguably
> popularized dog jokes with werewolves, and there
> are few things on this good earth that raise my ire
> more than werewolves being reduced to dog jokes
> or dog-people. Regardless, I do not dislike this
> movie in itself. It tells a fun story with a good
> moral. Unfortunately, however, I still feel we have
> it to blame for much of the infuriatingly comical
> portrayals of werewolves after its creation, and
> the encouragement of audiences to think of
> werewolves essentially as humanoid dogs,
> something to which werewolves should never be
> reduced.

Teen Wolf. MTV. New York, NY, 2011-. Television.

> Initially a guilty pleasure of mine, I eventually

took to shamelessly enjoying this series. The first season is the only one that is truly great and approaches perfect in its portrayal of werewolves, especially by my very particular standards. The seasons afterward vary in quality (the second season, for instance, is awful), but there are redeeming episodes throughout. The first season is an absolute must-watch. The introduction of and focus upon so many other fictional creatures drags the show down continually from the moment season one ends. My recommendation is to watch season one, which is truly an exceptional piece of werewolf-centric media, and then end it there.

Werewolf of London. Dir. Stuart Walker. Perf. Henry Hull and Valerie Hobson. Universal Pictures, 1935. DVD.

Predictable, today, to anyone familiar with werewolf and horror tropes, but probably a good enough movie during its time period. Still, not a favorite of mine. I don't recommend it.

The Wolf Man. Dir. George Waggner. Perf. Lon Chaney, Jr. and

Evelyn Ankers. Universal Pictures, 1941. DVD.

> Despite whatever small qualms I may have with this film, I cannot deny its incredible influence, and it is a very enjoyable, classic movie. A must-watch for anyone in the field; to not watch it is to not be at all informed on where nearly all modern werewolf concepts originated.

Wolf Blood. Dir. George Chesebro. Perf. George Chesebro and Roy Watson. Lee-Bradford Corporation, 1925. Internet Archive. Web. 20 Dec. 2016. <https://archive.org/details/WolfBlood1925>.

> A strange and hard to find film, as I am unsure for how long the provided link will function. If you cannot find it, do not worry yourself extensively; it is not worth it.

World of Warcraft: Cataclysm [Video game]. (2010). Blizzard Entertainment.

> Unfortunately, the worgen as a playable race were very halfhearted in multiple ways; for instance, they have extremely limited customization

choices (especially male worgen) compared to every other race, and Blizzard has made little to no effort to improve upon this; this lack of customization was thoroughly highlighted by the release of the playable pandaren and even the supposed extension to character customization options. Also, the entirety of their racial starting zone has terrible lore, as covered in the body of this work. Regardless, the worgen – even snubbed – still have an overall good if undersized design (despite having no ability to howl or to use their claws and teeth in combat) and receive the excellent Running Wild and Two Forms abilities. Play the expansion pack *Legion* and watch the cutscene of Genn Greymane in Stormheim if you want to see the worgen as the playable race should have been.

Zevon, Warren. "Werewolves of London." *Excitable Boy.* Asylum Records, 1978. CD.

A very fun and good song.

THE WEREWOLF: PAST AND FUTURE

Secondary Sources

Baring-Gould, Sabine. *The Book of Were-Wolves*. 1865. Radford, VA: Wilder Publications, 2007. Print.

> Although undeniably one of the most-used and most useful sources for werewolf folklore and history, Baring-Gould nonetheless includes a considerable amount of strange and overall irrelevant information, particularly where madmen are concerned, and frequently shows his bias. Regardless, this is an absolute must-have for anyone in the field and probably my favorite secondary source on werewolf legends. I have published my own edition of this book now, so I certainly recommend that one, as I included my own annotations, translations, improved formatting, and more.

Beresford, Matthew. *The White Devil: The Werewolf in European Culture*. London, England: Reaktion, 2013. Print.

> An excellent book on werewolves, even if some of the information seems irrelevant to the study of

lycanthropy itself, particularly the earliest chapters on prehistory. Regardless, all of it is good information, and Beresford is very skilled at presenting his findings and argument. Very highly recommended. Also be sure to look up his publications on other folklore, such as vampires.

Blécourt, Willem de. "A Journey to Hell: Reconsidering the Livonian "Werewolf"." *Magic, Ritual, and Witchcraft* 2.1 (2007): 49-67. *Project MUSE*. Web. 2 Oct. 2015. <http://muse.jhu.edu.ezproxy.lib.vt.edu/journals/magic_ritual_and_witchcraft/v002/2.1.deblecourt.html>.

A good and useful article, overall.

Douglas, Adam. *The Beast Within: A History of the Werewolf.* New York, NY: Avon, 1994. Print.

A decent book, though some of his arguments seem questionable at times. Recommended, if you can find a copy, but there are other books to turn to if you cannot. It is not a personal favorite or terribly useful, and some of its information is very questionable.

Garlipp, P., T. Gödecke-Koch, D. E. Dietrich, and H.
Haltenhof. "Lycanthropy – Psychopathological and
Psychodynamical Aspects." *Acta Psychiatrica Scandinavica*
109.1 (2004): 19-22. *Wiley Online Library*. Web.
<http://onlinelibrary.wiley.com/doi/10.1046/j.1600-
0447.2003.00243.x/abstract>.

> An interesting study on clinical lycanthropy and
> useful in defining the way in which doctors today
> think of it.

Jones, Stephen, ed. *The Mammoth Book of Wolf Men: The
Ultimate Werewolf Anthology*. Philadelphia, PA: Running
Book, 2009. Print.

> A decent anthology, though as mentioned in the
> body of this work, it is largely a collection of
> stereotypical werewolf horror, with an
> introduction to highlight as much. I don't care
> much for it or, really, the stories it contains.

Lopez, Barry. *Of Wolves and Men*. 1978. New York, NY: Scribner,
2004. Print.

> An absolutely outstanding book and a great study
> into how humans think of the wolf, both

realistically and mythologically. An absolute must-have.

Morley, Henry, ed. "The History of Reynard the Fox: William Caxton's English Translation of 1481." *Early Prose Romances*. Vol. 4. London: George Routledge and Sons, 1889. Web. <http://bestiary.ca/etexts/morley1889/morley%20-%20history%20of%20reynard%20the%20fox.pdf>.

A useful resource, especially for those interested in medieval works.

Otten, Charlotte F., ed. *A Lycanthropy Reader: Werewolves in Western Culture*. Syracuse, NY: Syracuse UP, 1986. Print.

Perhaps the single most useful and best-written work on werewolf legends, Otten has compiled an excellent reader of many works on lycanthropy that anyone in the field should own. She also includes an excellent introduction. Unquestionably a must-have, even to those only interested in lycanthropy as fans of werewolf media. It is the most treasured book in my collection on werewolf folklore.

Sconduto, Leslie A. *Metamorphoses of the Werewolf: A Literary Study from Antiquity Through the Renaissance.* Jefferson, NC: McFarland, 2008. Print.

>A good book, and an interesting literary study of various werewolf works. However, some of her information requires at least double-checking across several sources in order to confirm its accuracy.

Summers, Montague. *Werewolf.* 1933. Mansfield Centre, CT: Martino, 2012. Print.

>A must-have for anyone in the field, though Summers occasionally contradicts himself and makes sweeping, untrue statements (such as stating, correctly, in one chapter that werewolves have tails and then declaring that werewolves do not have tails; note that having a tail is, in folklore, considered a defining aspect of a werewolf). Summers is perhaps more extensive in providing useful information on werewolves and werewolf legends even than Baring-Gould,

instead of focusing on madmen – however, he always discusses werewolves with his bias that they are real and are related to Satan. Best used as a source of good sources to be cross-checked in various ways, as Summers himself cannot always be trusted.

Acknowledgements & Thanks

While werewolves and everything to do with them – and the very arguments I shall present here – have dwelt in my mind even since my childhood, this study was written as my thesis for a Master of Arts degree in English from Virginia Polytechnic Institute and State University (Virginia Tech), where it was reviewed multiple times, criticized, and ultimately approved. I defended this thesis before a committee of distinguished, extremely talented, and knowledgeable professors. I considerably exceeded the page requirements with my passion for the subject and the field, but I was not reprimanded. It is with deepest gratitude that I thank *Dr. Shoshana Milgram Knapp*, *Dr. Peter W. Graham*, and *Dr. Karen Swenson* for their endless support, advice, and guidance throughout my undergraduate and graduate careers, including on this thesis, and their continued support of my academic career and my fiction-writing pursuits. I cannot emphasize enough how much they have aided and inspired me in multiple ways reading and responding to my writing, as well as providing me constant encouragement. I also acknowledge the great aid put forth by my family: my mother, Mary; my father, Jack; and my amazing brothers, Justin and Ryan, all of whom have always supported me in every endeavor I have undertaken.

Thank you, all of you, for everything. This would not have been possible without you. Further special thanks goes to all my patrons, as well as the following individuals for their generous support throughout my various creative endeavors:

Ajestice
Alex
Sonja "Tafferling" Bauernfeind
Jared Buniel
Lacey
Kyle "Ambad" Smith
Valerie "Coop"

For updates on my future work and information on my previous publications, novels and otherwise, be sure to visit me online at:

WWW.MAVERICKWEREWOLF.COM

Scan this QR code to sign up for my newsletter! You'll find details at the link.

Please also consider picking up some of my fiction and giving it a try. I promise you won't regret it.

Other Works

I am always publishing more books, so be sure to look me up online and follow me on social media for more werewolf books, both fiction and nonfiction, and other genres!

The following list is up to date as of the year this book was published and should not be taken as current.

Set in the world of Wulfgard

My works of Wulfgard take place along a particular timeline. They are best experienced in order, but they can be read in any order at all, or you can just start with *Knightfall*.

- *The Tomb of Ankhu*
- *The Hunt Never Ends*
- *Tales of Wulfgard, Volume I*
- *The Prophecy of the Six, Book I: Knightfall* (rerelease and major revision coming 2024)

Nonfiction/Academic/Research works

- *The Werewolf: Past and Future – Lycanthropy's Lost History and Modern Devolution*
- *The Book of Were-Wolves* by Sabine Baring-Gould, edited by Maegan A. Stebbins
- *Werewolf Facts: A Guidebook to Folklore vs Popular Culture* (coming soon)

Printed in Great Britain
by Amazon